What Parsifal Saw

Tom Artin

FreeScholarPress

ISBN: 0692705449
ISBN-13: 978-0692705445

Cover Illustration: Arthur Hacker, "The Temptation of Sir Percival," 1894, Leeds City Art Gallery.

For my sister and my brother

Karin

&

Mike

CONTENTS

ACKNOWLEDGMENTS

Thanks to David Beisel
for insight and encouragement
en route to this study,
over coffee in Piermont
long past the time
the girls were looking
to close up.

I: Prelude:

The Unconscious in the Creation of Art

"Den unerforschlich tief
geheimnisvollen Grund,
wer macht der Welt ihn kund?"
Tristan und Isolde, II, 3

A newcomer to the psychoanalytic worldview could scarcely find a more lucid introduction to the position of the unconscious in the topography of mind than Stefan Zweig's chapter "The World of the Unconscious" in his 1931 encomium on Sigmund Freud's synthesizing theoretical achievement.[1] He illustrates using the proverbial iceberg, whose visible tip above the ocean's surface represents but a fraction of the actual mass of mostly hidden ice; just so, the bulk of mental life lies below the surface, and is unconscious. Moreover, whereas we intuitively regard conscious mental activity as primary and predominant, Zweig notes that Freud "stresses emphatically: all mental acts are initially unconscious events; those that become conscious represent neither a different nor a hierarchically superior genus; rather, their passing into consciousness is simply an attribute."[2] Not only is the unconscious not subordinate to consciousness, it is on the contrary the fundament of mental activity, very much like Schopenhauer's unconscious will.

[1] Stefan Zweig, *Die Heilung durch den Geist. Mesmer – Mary Baker Eddy – Freud,* (Leipzig, 1931).
[2] Stefan Zweig, *Über Sigmund Freud,* (Frankfurt, 1998), p. 45, my trans.

"The unconscious is by no means the detritus of mental life, but rather itself its elemental stuff, of which only a tiny fragment reaches the illumined plane of consciousness. This major unseen portion, the so-called unconscious, is by no means thereby rendered moribund or inactive. Its effect is in actuality just as alive and active on our thinking and feeling; it represents perhaps the more vital part of our mental existence."[3]

If we apply this basic insight to the interpretation of works of art, we see that apparent meanings flickering across their surfaces are likewise at best partial, whether we are in pursuit of a work's genesis in the imagination of the artist, or its reception in the minds of its audience. This is not to suggest that unconscious meanings displace conscious ones, any more than unconscious motives and intentions—brought to light in an analytic session, let us say—negate manifest behavior in real life. The tip of an iceberg, and the mass of ice below the surface, after all, constitute an integral whole whose parts exist in a functional relation to one another. If as critics we excavate unconscious meanings in Wagner's *Ring*, for example, we are not declaring what *The Ring really* means, but what it *also* means. Multiple meanings of a work of art are layered, ranging from the apparent to the occult, and though when spelled out in linear fashion they might seem contradictory, by a deeper, inherent logic they are yoked organically together and are

[3] *Ibid.*, p. 47, my trans.

complementary.[4]

In this context, we must affirm the fundamental identity of any work of art and its meaning. At bottom, a work of art *is* its meaning. That is, the work of art itself is its immaterial conception materialized, its essence realized, the ideational manifested in palpable aesthetic form. The audience (or viewer, or reader) is free either to ponder and intellectualize over the realized work of art, or simply to experience it intuitively, to take it in, to be as it were washed over by it, confident that the aesthetic experience is infused with meaning, whether or not such meaning be converted into articulable thoughts.

Parsifal is a work that invariably leaves its audience deeply moved, if not transformed, whether or not conclusions are reached as to its meaning. That it *has* profound meaning is never in doubt. But the exact nature of that meaning often is. Is *Parsifal* a Christian work? A Buddhist work? How are we to understand the enigmatic formula, "Erlösung dem Erlöser?"[5] Is Kundry an agent of good or evil? How does compassion effect redemption? What exactly is the Grail?

Even after his acrimonious break with Wagner, Nietzsche, contemptuous of what he viewed as pandering to maudlin Christianity in *Parsifal,* nevertheless wrote of his first experience of the music, ". . . From a purely aesthetic point of view, has Wagner ever written anything better? The

---

[4] Cf. Tom Artin, *The Wagner Complex,* (Free Scholar Press, 2012). This book lays out a rationale for the applicability of Freud's theoretical schemes to Wagner's work in particular, see pp. 1-33.

[5] Redemption to the Redeemer.

supreme psychological awareness and certainty with respect to what is to be said, expressed, communicated here, the most concise and direct form to that end, every nuance of feeling condensed to the epigrammatic; a clarity of music as descriptive art that puts us in mind of a sublimely chased shield, and finally a lofty and extraordinary feeling, experience, spiritual event in the essence of the music, that does Wagner the highest honor . . . We get something comparable to it in Dante, but nowhere else. Has any painter ever depicted so melancholy a look of love as Wagner does in the final accents of his Prelude?"[6]

To his musical colleague and fellow Dresden conspirator August Röckel, Wagner had written years before on August 23, 1856 from Zürich, "How can an artist expect that what he has felt intuitively should be perfectly realized by others, seeing that he himself feels in the presence of his work, if it is true Art, that he is confronted by a riddle, about' which he too might have illusions, just as another might?" Surely Wagner himself must, to a degree at least, have felt confronted by such a riddle in *Parsifal*, a work whose meaning inspires debate to the present day. As Ulrike Kienzle opens her essay on its religious dimensions, "Wagner's Parsifal poses a riddle that is hard to solve." Of the work's essentially "sacred" nature there can be no question, she avers. "But what form of the sacred are we dealing with here?"[7]

---

[6] Friedrich Nietzsche to Peter Gast, January 21, 1887, my trans.
[7] Ulrike Kienzle, "*Parsifal* and Religion: A Christian Music Drama?" in William Kinderman & Katherine R. Syer, eds., *A Companion to Wagner's Parsifal*, (Camden House, 2005), p. 81.

Perhaps the essential experience of *Parsifal* is precisely this confrontation with an unanswered, or even unanswerable, question, "a riddle, wrapped in a mystery, inside an enigma," to borrow the Churchillian likeness. "Weißt du was du sahst?"[8] Gurnemanz asks Parsifal after he has witnessed the Grail ritual for the first time. Parsifal clutches at his heart and shakes his head. "Du bist doch eben nur ein Tor!"[9] Gurnemanz says, brusquely showing him the door.

With respect to the psychoanalytic exploration of *The Ring*, I wrote in *The Wagner Complex*, "this is a literary study, not a diagnostic one. I am not an analyst. Even if I were, it is doubtful that, lacking the 'patient's' associations—the crucial material of any analysis—such an endeavor would be particularly enlightening. My interpretations of Wagner's biography, to the extent they bear a psychoanalytic stamp, are aimed at elucidating the text and its genesis. My purpose is to coax out literary, not clinical meaning."[10] In the course of examining *Parsifal*, I have somewhat modified that view. It remains true that I am not a psychoanalyst, nor is it possible to lure Richard Wagner onto the analytic couch, nor—most important—do we have access to his stream of free associations that would constitute the Ariadne's thread of an analysis.

In the meantime, however, it occurs to me that what we do have is Wagner's verbal text of *Parsifal*.[11] The medium of

---

[8] "Do you know what you saw?"
[9] "You are just a fool then after all!"
[10] Artin, *op. cit.*, p. 32.
[11] As of *The Ring* and his other operas.

psychoanalysis is the verbal; mute emotions and fantasies are translated into words. Wagner's text, then, the words flowing from his mind onto the page, containing all his idiosyncratic nuances of wording and expression, and especially the many points on which the details of this text deviate from or elaborate his sources, is the transcript of a process not after all so entirely different from the free association of an analytic patient. Wagner's text, that is, can be regarded as a snapshot, as it were, of the state of his mind at the time of creation.

Accordingly, the present study approaches the text methodically (not to say doggedly), act by act, line by line, examining the texture of the verse and its thematic and symbolic content in the manner of an associative stream to see how the underlying unconscious symbolic and thematic structure is put together, stone by stone. The drama traces the soul's (or better, the psyche's) progress from the corporeal to the ethereal—from the rank concupiscence of Amfortas's wound and Kundry's voluptuous embrace to the sublime redemption accomplished by Parsifal's assumption of the Grail Kingship, the reuniting of holy spear and Grail, and the restoration of Eucharistic sustenance from the Grail.

In *The Ego and the Id*, Freud has written, "What biology and the fortunes of the human species have created and left as residue in the id, is appropriated by the ego in the formation of its ideal and recapitulated by the individual. In consequence of the process of its formation, the ego ideal displays the most extensive linkage to the phylogenetic acquisition, the archaic legacy of the individual. What belonged to the lowest depths in individual mental life, is transformed through formation of the ideal to the highest [manifestations] of the human spirit, according to our sense of values."[12] As we shall see, Freud's general schema nicely limns the narrative arc of *Parsifal*, even on the manifest level of the drama. The present study will search additionally below this manifest level for wider-reaching, though hidden, themes and motives, in an effort to elucidate the deeply enigmatic character of the work.

On a further methodological note, let me address and with any luck nip in the bud an objection that is otherwise likely to be made against the approach of this study. Though *Parsifal* is an opera (Wagner of course did not wish this term applied to what he designated grandiloquently a "*Bühnenweihfestspiel*"), *What Parsifal Saw* deals almost exclusively with the text, the "libretto," and only in passing with any musicological aspects of Wagner's work.[13]

"Libretto," first of all, is an inadequate and misleading term to apply to the texts of any of Wagner's works. Wagner is nearly unique in having written his own texts, always well in advance of committing a single note to paper. He referred to his texts as "Dichtungen," loosely "poems," or "literary works," and he often published these texts in formal readings and in print separately from his scores. As a "total artist," or "Gesamtkünstler," Wagner regarded himself a

---

[12] Sigmund Freud, *Das Ich und das Es, Werkausgabe in Zwei Bänden*, (Frankfurt, 1978), v. I, pp. 385-6, my trans.

[13] On the relative inapplicability of psychoanalytic interpretation to music, see *The Wagner Complex*, pp. 32-3.

poet as much as a musician. In the particular case of *Parsifal*—as he wrote Mathilde Wesendonck in early August, 1860—he actually seriously contemplated leaving the drama as a poem outright.

"Parzival[14] has been much awake in me again; I see ever more and clearly therein, when once it has all matured in me, that carrying out this poem ["Dichtung"] must become an unheard of joy for me. But this may well still take a good number of years! Also, I'd like for once to leave it simply as a poem." At this point in the decades-long chronology of *Parsifal*'s creation, Wagner regarded his "Parzivaldichtung" first of all as a literary work. It must seem entirely appropriate, then, to apply largely literary-critical approaches to its interpretation.

Translations from Wagner's German text are mine, as are those from Freud's writings and Martin Luther's German version of the Bible—these latter, so indicated in footnotes. I have found this necessary because available translations in English of all these texts, while for the most part not inaccurate *per se*, frequently obscure meanings and shadings clearly present in the original language—meanings and shadings that bear directly on the particular interpretive slant of this study, though they might not seem greatly significant to the general reader.

Particularly with regard to Wagner's German text, wherever it is not transparently rendered by its nearest English

---

[14] Wagner had not by the date of this letter (written from Paris) altered Wolfram von Eschenbach's spelling to "Parsifal."

equivalent, I have given the original at the foot of the page for comparison so the reader may judge the pertinence of my reading. Likewise, wherever I have quoted the German in my text, my English translation appears at the foot of the page.

Footnotes in this study, then, fall roughly into two categories: citation of sources and other scholarly additions to the main text of the study, and English or German versions of Wagner's or Luther's text quoted in the text above.

II. Weißt du was du sahst?

Parsifal displays prominently—which is to say, its action is informed and driven by—six principal themes:

- Ignorance—Parsifal as the pure fool, *der reine Tor*.
- Seeing—what Parsifal saw in the Grail Knights' ritual of uncovering the Grail.
- Maternal sacrifice—Herzeleide's seclusion in the forest to guard her son from the perils of knighthood; her death of a broken heart when he abandons her.
- Sex as perilous—Amfortas's wound, and Klingsor's threat to all knights who fall prey to his alluring flower-maidens.
- Seduction—Kundry's role as temptress of both Amfortas and Parsifal.
- Redemption through compassion.

The first of these themes, ignorance, appears in the opening moments of *Parsifal's* unfolding action. Gurnemanz inquires of the advance guard of Amfortas and his party about the king's condition, and hazards hopefully the guess that the healing herbs Gawain has won from afar have brought the king relief from his agony.

"You fancy that—you who know everything?!"[15] replies the second knight, almost reproachfully. No, ever more searing pain has soon returned. Gawain's "cunning and daring"[16] have proven fruitless. Gurnemanz's vaunted wisdom is not so perfect after all. This singular gap in his otherwise comprehensive knowledge is in respect to Amfortas's incurable wound, the consequence of intercourse with Kundry.

"Fools, we, to hope for relief there, where only healing brings relief!"[17] Gurnemanz broods. Fleetingly, the figure of the fool, *der Tor*, so central to the entire work, and embodied in the person of Parsifal, is here introduced with the implication that "foolishness" is universal. This thematic idea is deepened when he muses, "He can be helped by only one thing—only the one [person]!"[18] for these words are set to a fragment of the "fool" leitmotif—in German, the *Torenspruch* motif—which in its complete form will carry the formula that can be considered the philosophical legend of the entire work: "Durch Mitleid wissend, der reine Tor."[19]

"He can be helped by only . . . the one!"

"Then tell us who that is!"[20] pleads the second knight. But Gurnemanz remains oddly silent, and abruptly changes the subject: "See to the bath!" he orders. Immediately, the two

15 "Das wähnest du, der doch alles weiß?"
16 "List und Kühnheit"
17 "Toren wir, auf Lind'rung da zu hoffen, wo einzig Heilung lindert!"
18 "ihm hilft nur eines—nur der Eine!"
19 "Enlightened through compassion, the pure fool."
20 "So nenn' uns den!"

squires announce the approach of Kundry, as though in answer to the knight's question. Is Kundry, then, "the one?" Looking ahead, the more apparent answer will prove to be Parsifal, the pure fool. Yet Parsifal's agency as healer of "the wound that will not close," restorer of the holy spear, and redeemer of the Grail Knighthood is itself enabled by Kundry, in more ways than one—a duality to which we shall return.

The knights and squires witness Kundry's approach astride her staggering mare. The First Knight opines that she must come bearing important news—or information[21]—a service Gurnemanz tells his audience it is her habit to perform for the Grail Knights. Whenever they are "at a loss"[22] how to send intelligence[23] to their brothers in arms in far off lands, Kundry somehow appears as if out of nowhere to carry their messages. What she bears in this instance in Act I is Arabian balm (or balsam) to apply to Amfortas's wound.

Gurnemanz asks whence she has brought it. "From further off than you can think,"[24] she replies. And then, obscurely, "Ask no further."[25] Why such a prohibition from a person who is a regular messenger, a conveyor of information? The insinuation may be that Kundry's source for her healing balm is illicit. Whatever the case, though, the continuing

---

[21] The German word is "Kunde," which could mean either.
[22] "ratlos," literally, "without counsel."
[23] "Kunde"
[24] "Von Weiter her als du denken kannst," which might also be translated, "From further off than you can imagine."
[25] "Fragt nicht weiter."

theme here—still *sotto voce*—is knowledge, intelligence gathered, and its obverse, ignorance.

Now Amfortas is borne in on a litter *en route* to his regular cleansing/healing bath in the holy lake. He alludes to the previous "night's wild agonizing pain,"[26] but his suffering has eased with the "morning's sylvan beauty." He now introduces in its complete form one of *Parsifal's* leading themes, musical and semantical: "Durch Mitleid wissend, der reine Tor." The "pure fool" is the figure through whom alone Amfortas can hope for healing, and the Knighthood, redemption.

Gurnemanz hands him the "secret vessel"[27] containing the balsam. (This exotic vessel parallels and anticipates the sacred and miraculous vessel that is the Grail itself.) When Amfortas learns Kundry has brought it, apparently unaware that she is the "terribly beautiful woman"[28] who had seduced him in Klingsor's domains, rendering him vulnerable to the wound from the holy spear in the sorcerer's hand, he asks, "Must I once more thank you?"

Kundry barks, "Not thanks!—Ha ha, What will it help? Not thanks! Away! Away! Into the bath!"[29] Kundry's duplicitous nature—treacherous seductress and penitent servant—(though still veiled in obscurity) underlies this cryptic statement. Her striking duality is a manifest instance

---

26 "wilder Schmerzensnacht"

27 "heimliches Gefäß"

28 "furchtbar schönes Weib"

29 "Nicht Dank!—Haha! Was wird es helfen? Nicht Dank! Fort, fort! Ins Bad!"

of the Madonna/whore trope, first identified by Freud[30] and elaborated since by many other writers in myriad variations. As an Oedipal fantasy, the trope splits the introjected mother image into forbidden object, and sexual object available to all, *even the son*.

Amfortas signals his entourage to continue to the lake, leaving Gurnemanz behind with the young squires and Kundry sprawled on the ground. "What are you doing lying there like a wild animal?" one of the squires asks.

"Are not the animals holy here?" is Kundry's reply, set to the pervasive motif of the Dresden Amen.

"Yes. But whether you be holy, we just don't know yet," answers the squire, tying this exchange to the theme of knowing and unknowing.

Another squire adds, "I suspect she will totally ruin the master with her magic juice [*Zaubersaft*]."[31] Meant is the Arabian balm, or balsam, although "Saft" is a peculiar word. Let us tuck away for future reference what is plausibly an echo (consciously or not) of Mephistopheles's insistence that Faust sign his infernal contract not in ink but blood: "Blut ist ein ganz besonderer Saft."[32]

---

[30] Sigmund Freud, "A Special Type of Choice of Object Made by Men," *Standard Edition*, (London, 1910), v. XI, pp. 163-176.

[31] "Mit ihrem Zaubersaft, wähn' ich, wird sie den Meister vollends verderben."

[32] "Blood is an altogether extraordinary juice," Goethe, *Faust I*, 1,740, my trans.

Gurnemanz, apparently unaware that Kundry remains secretly in thrall to Klingsor, tries to explain her dual nature to the squires by suggesting that though she may well harbor some heinous sin in her past, perhaps she is now atoning for it by way of service to the Grail Knighthood.

One of the squires unwittingly hits the nail on the head. "So is it perhaps that guilt of hers that has brought us such woe?"

Misconstruing the thrust of the squire's question, Gurnemanz muses, "Yes, often when she has long stayed away from us, then it's true, misfortune befell us." He turns to Kundry and asks, "Hey! You! Listen to me and tell us: where were you roaming at that time when our Lord lost the spear? Why did you not aid us then?" Gurnemanz is treading perilously close to the truth; on that occasion Kundry was in fact engaged in intercourse with Amfortas, enabling both the theft of the holy spear and Amfortas's incurable wound at Klingsor's hand.

Kundry's oblique reply: "I . . . never help."

And the squire poses the trenchant, ironic challenge, "If she is so true, so daring in our defense, then send *her* after the lost spear!"

Gurnemanz's reply is dark. "That is something else: it is forbidden to each."[33] What is the nature of this prohibition?

---

33 "Das ist ein and'res: jedem ist's verwehrt."

Who has imposed it, and by what power? Gurnemanz goes on to apostrophize the spear, "O wunden-wundervoller, heiliger Speer!" This first attribute is not easily rendered in English. It involves a word-play on "wundervoll" ("wonderful, marvelous"), but the paradoxical yoking of "wunden" and "wunder" (wound/wonder) suggests more. The holy spear is the spear with which Longinus pierced Jesus's side as he hung on the cross; that wound itself works wonders. In some legends, Longinus was said to have been blind; some of the blood from Jesus's wound fell onto his eyes, and his blindness was cured. More important, the blood collected by Joseph of Arimathea in the vessel that will prove to be the Holy Grail is identical to the blood of Christ transubstantiated in the Eucharist. The holy spear, that is, works wonders in the very act of wounding.

Gurnemanz goes on to lament, " I saw you brandished in most unholy hand!"[34] The imagery of the hand assumes pregnancy further on in Gurnemanz's narrative of Klingsor when he relates how the magician, unable to curb his erotic impulses,[35] mastered them by self-castration: "On himself he laid the sinner's hand."[36] Shortly thereafter, Gurnemanz tells the squires, "the spear is now in Klingsor's hand; if he can wound even holy ones with it, he imagines he has

[34] "Ich sah dich schwingen von unheilgster Hand!"

[35] Gurnemanz says Klingsor wished to atone for his obscure sin, "doch wollt' er büßen nun, ja heilig werden." Wagner's use of "heilig" is ambiguous, perhaps intentionally. Though "heilig" means "holy," its original meaning is "healthy, whole and uninjured. See Victor Henle, *Wagners Wörter: ein Lexikon*, (Berlin-München, 2011), p. 59.

[36] "an sich legt' er die Frevlerhand."

already as good as firmly wrested the Grail from us."[37] And at the conclusion of Act II, when Klingsor hurls the spear at Parsifal, Wagner notes in his stage direction that Parsifal, "Grasps the spear with his hand"—a gratuitous specificity: what else would he grasp the spear with?

The holy spear in *Parsifal* has a widely acknowledged phallic character; in the context of this description of Klingsor, the circumlocution "an sich legt' er die Frevlerhand" is as suggestive of masturbation as of castration, particularly since masturbation is a far easier, more benign, and routine way of controlling erotic impulses than the drastic and perverse mutilation of self-castration.

That masturbation was a matter of consequence (not to say an obsession) with Wagner is manifest in the fateful and notorious letter he posted in the fall of 1877 to Dr. Eiser, a physician Nietzsche had consulted in Frankfurt.[38] Nietzsche

---

[37] "der Speer ist nun in Klingsors Hand; kann er selbst Heilige mit dem verwunden, den Gral auch wähnt' er fest schon uns entwunden!" The dual, complementary imagery of spear and Grail will be explored in due course.

[38] On this incident (which Nietzsche regarded as a "mortal insult"), see the following: Martin Gregor-Dellin, *Richard Wagner: His Life, His Work, His Century*, (New York, 1983), pp. 451-458; Joachim Köhler, *Nietzsche & Wagner: A Lesson in Subjugation*, (New Haven, 1998), pp. 139-157; Joachim Köhler, *Zarathustra's Secret*, (New Haven, 2002), pp. 97-109; Bryan Magee, *The Tristan Chord: Wagner and Philosophy*, (New York, 2000), pp. 330-38.

On the wide-spread and quasi obsessional fixation on the purported deleterious effects of masturbation, see Thomas W. Laqueur, *Solitary Sex: A Cultural History of Masturbation*, (New York, 2003), and Sue Prideaux, *Strindberg: A Life*, (New Haven, 2012), pp. 50-1.

For a typical example of the anti-masturbatory literature wide-spread throughout 19th c. Europe (the book that so deeply tormented

had suffered most of his adult life with general ill-health, including migraines, failing eye-sight, and intestinal disorders.[39] Over the course of 4 days in October, Dr. Eiser and an ophthalmologist, Dr. Krüger, examined Nietzsche fully, and determined that in addition to a chronic inflammatory condition in his central nervous system, he was probably going blind. Nietzsche reported these results in general terms to the Wagners at Bayreuth, prompting Wagner to write Dr. Eiser directly, advising him that Nietzsche's physical problems were doubtless the results of chronic masturbation. This indiscretion was not in and of itself the proximal cause of the break between the two, but Wagner's "mortal insult"[40] now rendered the breach irreconcilable.

Strindberg), see, Sixtus Carl von Kappf, *Warnung eines Jugendfreundes vor dem gefährlichen Jugendfeind oder Belehrung über geheime Sünden, ihre Folgen, Heilung und Verhütung durch Beispiele aus dem Leben erläuteret und der Jugend und ihren Erziehern ans Herz gelegt*, (Stuttgart, 1844). In English, von Kappf's title reads, *Warning from a Friend of Youth Against the Most Dangerous Enemy of Youth, or Instruction on Secret Sins, their Consequences, Cures, and Prevention, Elucidated through Examples Taken from Life, and Fervently Urged upon Youth and its Instructors.*

[39] Most of these symptoms have long since been attributed to the syphilis that ultimately took Nietzsche's sanity.

[40] "eine tödtliche Beleidigung,:" as Nietzsche later characterized it in a letter to Franz Overbeck, February 22, 1883, shortly following Wagner's death in Venice. "*Wagner* war bei weitem der *vollste* Mensch, den ich kennenlernte, und in *diesem* Sinne habe ich seit sechs Jahren eine große Entbehrung gelitten. *Aber* es gibt etwas zwischen uns beiden wie eine tödliche Beleidigung; und es hätte furchtbar kommen können, wenn er noch länger gelebt haben würde." "*Wagner* was by far the most complete human being I ever met, and in *this* sense I have suffered a great deprivation the past six years. *But* there is something like a mortal insult between us, and it might have come to something terrible had he lived any longer," my trans.

To recognize that a complex of feelings, fantasies, and prohibitions surrounding masturbation underlies the imagery of Klingsor's self-castration is important for a number of reasons. First, we have to pose the general question how and why a fanciful narrative such as *Parsifal,* set in the Middle Ages, and composed as it is of all sorts of magically inflated elements remote from the reality of bourgeois life in 19th century Germany (or 21st century America, for that matter), is taken seriously by a modern audience. What leads to its assimilation, not just as a fanciful fairy-tale set to sublime music, but as a profound parable of human nature?

The answer is that each of the magical and inflated elements refers—through the medium of symbolism—to a more mundane, quotidian fact of life. Ultimately, the whole of *Parsifal* is a representation of the reality of the human situation. In the case of Klingsor's self-mutilation, for instance, we must be struck by just how bizarre an act it is if taken on its face, and while not perhaps absolutely unheard of in real life, it is still so rare an occurrence as not to impinge on our actual lives at all. Quite the opposite is true of masturbation, of course; taboo notwithstanding, nothing could be more quotidian or normal.

Stefan Zweig was in the habit of sending Freud his writings as they were issued, to which Freud frequently offered his commentary in numerous letters. In response to Zweig's novella *Verwirrung der Gefühle*,[41] Freud wrote the following, which will prove worth quoting at length:

> "I truly believe, however, that these three novellas—more precisely, two of them—are masterpieces. The first of course was already known to me . . . You had awakened my particular interest because it admits of an analytic interpretation, or even demands such, and because in [the course of] communication with you I became convinced that you knew nothing of this secret meaning, while at the same time having given expression to it in a perfect disguise. You probably do not recognize such an interpretive possibility, perhaps you abhor it, but I cannot dismiss it, and this time I have received a far more comprehensive [view of it]. Analysis[42] suggests that the great, seemingly inexhaustible wealth of problems and situations treated by the writer can be traced back to a small number of 'Ur-motifs,' rooted mostly in the material of repressed experiences of childhood mental life, so that these poetic fictions correspond to disguised, euphemized, sublimated revisions of those childhood fantasies. This may be shown especially readily in the first novella. Stated bluntly without sugar-coating, the unconscious core seems repulsive. The motif is that of the mother who introduces the son to sexual intercourse sacrificing her own person in order to rescue him from the dangers of masturbation, which to the child appear hugely life-threatening. Such a

[41] "Confusion of Feelings."

[42] Presumably Freud means psychoanalysis.

> fantasy is remembered consciously by many from their own years of puberty. It is never absent from the unconscious. It also constitutes the basis of all fictions of redemption—Wagner's operas, for example. In fictional treatment, masturbation—which is entirely unsuitable for use—must be replaced with something else; in your novella, play is the proper substitute.
>
> The compulsiveness, irresistibility, the relapses despite the firmest resolutions, the threat to life are direct features of the old pattern; the first designation masturbation was given in the nursery was 'playing'—a dangerous game, the child was told, from which one went mad, or died—and the emphasis on the hands and their activity achieved with such uncanny mastery by you is downright revelatory. In masturbation, after all, the hands effect their genital function. In your novella, the young player's role as son is indicated so unmistakably that it is hard to believe you had not pursued a conscious intention. I know, however, that this was not the case, and that you allowed your unconscious to be at work."[43]

Freud's letter is illuminating in numerous ways, not least his comment *en passant* concerning Wagner's operas.[44] First, he

---

[43] Sigmund Freud to Stefan Zweig, September 4, 1926, collected in *Stefan Zweig über Sigmund Freud: Porträt, Briefwechsel, Gedenkworte,* (Frankfurt am Main, 1989), pp. 138-9, my trans.

[44] On Freud's knowledge of Wagner's works, see Cora L. Diaz de Chumaceiro, "Richard Wagner's Life and Music: What Freud Knew," in

recognizes unconscious intention in the creation of Zweig's work, calling to mind Wagner's letter to Röckel, cited above. Though Zweig may well have been unaware of the psychoanalytic dimension of his characters' interactions, their "secret meaning," in composing the work, Freud assures him his depiction is clinically sound, though he might well "abhor it." Next, he identifies the narrative template of Zweig's novella as one of the "small number of 'Ur-motifs'" that manifest themselves time and again in literature and drama. In this case it is "that of the mother who introduces the son to sexual intercourse sacrificing her own person in order to rescue him from the dangers of masturbation, which to the child appear hugely life-threatening." The infantile fantasy that masturbation entails grave mortal danger informs the sublimated fiction of *Parsifal,* infusing it with a seriousness that is far from apparent in a mere *precis* of the libretto.

This "Ur-motif" is, Freud writes, "the basis of all fictions of redemption," including Wagner's operas.[45] Redemption—Freud's word, like Wagner's, is "Erlösung"—constitutes not just a major motif in *Parsifal;* it is in fact the narrative goal toward which the entire drama makes its determined, leisurely way. This is a matter to be elucidated in due course.

Gurnemanz concludes his exposition of Klingsor's story by

Feder, Karmel, & Pollock, *Psychoanalytic Explorations in Music, Second Series,* (Madison, CT., 1993), pp. 249-278.

[45] Note that Freud's subject here is not Wagner's operas *per se;* the comment is a casual aside, rather out of the blue, which only bolsters its pertinence to *Parsifal.*

recounting the origin of what we designated the philosophical legend of the story: "Durch Mitleid wissend, der reine Tor; harre sein den ich erkor." The squires intone an ethereal echo, but reach only the word "Tor," when, as though foreshadowing in the same way as earlier the sudden appearance of Kundry seemed almost a reply to the squire's demand, "So nenn' uns den!" Parsifal's entrance is now heralded by the squires and knights who lead in the callow culprit caught shooting a wild swan with an arrow. Parsifal is indeed a fool by virtue of his wide-eyed ignorance and inexperience, and will prove to be the "pure fool" ("der reine Tor") of the hallowed prophecy only after passing through a long and arduous gauntlet of trials.

The swan's wound, its white feathers "still thick with [red] blood."[46] parallels the wound of Amfortas: "the wound that will never close!"[47] as Gurnemanz mused earlier. Parsifal's arrow, then, is a figural echo of the holy spear. This image of blood "darkly spotting the [swan's] snow-white feathers,"[48] introduces the blood motif that will pervade Wagner's "stage-consecrating-festival-play."

"What did the loyal swan do to you?"[49] Gurnemanz chides Parsifal. The swan was flying in search of its mate; circling the lake together they would have consecrated the bath. This image of male and female swan, paired as a functional unit, will also prove to be an important one, prefiguring the union of Parsifal and Kundry.

---

[46] "da starrt noch das Blut"
[47] "Die Wunde ist's, die nie sich schließen will!"
[48] "das Schneegefieder dunkel befleckt"
[49] "Was tat dir der treue Schwan?"

Gurnemanz's question hits its mark. Parsifal, stricken with remorse, breaks his bow and tosses his arrows aside. Now Gurnemanz poses a series of personal questions, each of which Parsifal answers with a profession of ignorance. He did not know it was a sin to kill the swan; nor where he comes from; nor who his father is; nor who sent him this way; nor so much as his name.

In musing curiously, "as dumb as this one, I've not thought[50] anyone till now but Kundry!" Gurnemanz links Parsifal with Kundry. In what sense is Kundry dumb? In fact, only a few lines further on Gurnemanz tells Parsifal that Kundry has spoken the truth, "for Kundry never lies, though she has seen much."[51] She is certainly resourceful. The only manifest evidence that could be taken as a sign of unintelligence are her periodic and close to incoherent moans and outbursts. It may emerge, however, that she shares in the "pure foolishness" that will stamp Parsifal as the pure fool, the redeemer, prophesied by the Grail.

To Gurnemanz's question what, after all, he *does* know, Parsifal's reply is pointedly singular. He has a mother. Herzeleide is her name. Kundry fills in the story for us (further evidence she is not actually "dumb"). His mother gave birth to the child, fatherless because Gamuret had been slain in knightly battle. To protect him from the same mortal dangers,[52] his mother had raised him in the wilderness to be

---

[50] "erfand bisher ich Kundry nur!" For this usage of "erfinden" see *Wagners Wörter*, p. 33.

[51] "Was tat dir das Weib! Es sagte wahr; denn nie lügt Kundry, doch sah sie viel."

[52] To be noted is an intriguing parallel between Parsifal's relation to his mother and Wagner's own childhood, about which he says in *Mein*

a fool—(fool she! comments Kundry archly).[53] In this narrative we recognize crucial elements of the literary motif identified by Freud: "The motif . . . of the mother who introduces the son to sexual intercourse sacrificing her own person in order to rescue him from the dangers of masturbation, which to the child appear hugely life-threatening." Kundry's narrative here does not explicitly include the "introduction to sexual intercourse" of Freud's Ur-motif, but that Oedipal dimension will become overt in the seduction scene of Act II, and we explore it further in that context.

Parsifal's perfect innocence is underscored by his naïve questions concerning good and evil. "Were those who threatened me bad? Who is good?"

To the latter, Gurnemanz replies, "Your mother, whom you abandoned, and who now frets and sorrows over you."

But Kundry delivers the decisive blow: "Her sorrow is past;

Leben: "my mother took the greatest care to prevent me from developing any taste whatever for the theatre." Similarly, regarding the field of music, "Oddly enough, I was the only child in our family who had not been given music lessons. This was probably due to my mother's anxiety to keep me away from any artistic interests of this kind in case they might arouse in me a longing for the theatre," my trans.
". . . meine Mutter [hielt] angelegentlich darauf, in mir nicht etwa auch Neigung für das Theater aufkommen zu lassen." And, "Denn, sonderbar genug, war ich der Einzige unter meinen Geschwistern, welcher keinen Klavierunterricht empfangen hatte, was ich wahrscheinlich der ängstlichen Sorge meiner Mutter verdankte, mir derlie künstlerische Uebungen, welche mir etwa Neigung zum Theater beibringen könnten, fern zu halten." *Mein Leben*, (München, 1911), pp. 17, 39.

[53] "in Öden erzog sie ihn zum Toren—Törin!" On Wagner's broad use of "Tor," see *Wagners Wörter*, p. 124.

his mother is dead!"

"Dead? . . . My . . . mother? Who says this?"

"I rode by and saw her dying," Kundry answers. "She bade me greet you, fool."

Gurnemanz restrains Parsifal, who, enraged, has seized Kundry by the throat. "What did the woman do to you?"[54] Gurnemanz chides, reprising the rhetorical question he had put to him over the slain swan, thereby thematically linking Kundry and the swan.

Kundry now repays Parsifal's violence with good, as Gurnemanz tells her (her demurral "I never do good" notwithstanding), by fetching water from a spring in a horn, sprinkling Parsifal with it as though in benediction, and giving him to drink, a gesture she will repeat in a bit of narrative symmetry in Act III. The drink Kundry now proffers the thirsting Parsifal ("Ich verschmachte!")[55] from the horn fashioned into a vessel foreshadows the Grail rite, of which Gurnemanz will tell the acolyte, "if you are pure, the Grail will now give you food and drink."[56] Gurnemanz attributes Kundry's selfless act to "the grace of the Grail."

The exhausted Kundry demurs, saying she never does good, and turns away, longing only for rest, sleep she thinks, then starts abruptly at the thought of dreams that are sure to haunt that sleep. Trembling, she retreats into the bush, and

---

[54] "Was tat dir das Weib?"

[55] "I thirst!" Though using a different word, Parsifal's plea probably echoes Christ's words on the cross, "Mich dürstet!" *John* 19:28.

[56] "Denn bist du rein, wird nun der Gral dich tränken und speisen."

sinks to the ground. "Futile resistance,"[57] she says, yielding to her fate, and then, anticipating the foreboding pronouncement with which Klingsor will open Act II, utters: "Die Zeit ist da."[58]

Gurnemanz assumes a paternal attitude, putting Parsifal's arm around his neck, his own arm supporting the younger man's body. "Now let me lead you to the sacred meal."

Here—brilliantly—Wagner puts into Parsifal's mouth the touchingly naïve query, "Who is the Grail?"[59] a question that elicits our own crucial interpretive inquiry, "*what* is the Grail?" Together, elder and youth stride mystically down that passage where (as though anticipating Einstein) "time . . . becomes space."

"Pay close attention now," Gurnemanz admonishes the neophyte, "and let me see: if you be a fool and pure, what knowledge may be granted you." Together, they observe the unfolding Grail ritual.

The Grail Knights file in and take their places around the feast table. In a sequential word play on "das Letzte

---

57 "Machtlose Wehr!"

58 "The time has come." This anticipation of Klingsor's pronouncement is additionally noteworthy in that it bears no apparent pertinence to the narrative context in which Kundry utters it. Midway in his extended plea that he be spared administration of the Grail ritual, Amfortas cries, "Die Stunde naht," "The hour draws near." In Act II, conjuring Kundry from her "death sleep," Klingsor says, "Meinem Banne wieder verfallen heut' zur rechten Zeit." "Once again in thrall to my spell at the right time." In Act III, anticipating the reenactment of the Grail ritual, Gurnemanz says, "Die Stund' ist da." "The hour has come." This motif of time will be further elucidated in our examination of Act II (below).

59 "Wer ist der Gral?"

Abendmahl" ("the Last Supper"), the Knights intone their somber, liturgical invocation of the rite. "To the Last Love-Supper, prepared day after day, though it should be for the last time it feed us today. The feast will be renewed for whoever delights in good deeds; he may approach the meal, receive the most sublime gift."[60]

To illuminate the underlying essential nature of Wagner's Grail, it will be useful to list its attributes abstracted from narrative context. The Grail is a vessel whose function is to contain blood: initially, the blood of Christ transubstantiated from wine at the Last Supper; then, the blood that flowed from Christ's side pierced as he hung on the Cross by the spear of Longinus. Unveiled and revealed, Wagner's Grail glows with an intense, ethereal scarlet effusion that floods the entire temple with blood-colored light and effects the transubstantiation of the wine and bread at the Grail Knights' feast table into the Eucharistic blood and body of the Redeemer.

A further attribute of Wagner's Grail is its periodicity. Normally concealed, it is periodically brought out for the reenactment of the ritual. Uncovered, its insubstantial "bleeding" provokes renewed actual bleeding from Amfortas's wound. He cries out, "I feel the sacred vessel's . . . most holy fount of blood pour into my heart: the surge

---

[60] "Zum *letzten* Liebes*mahle,* gerüstet Tag für Tag, gleich ob zum *letzten Male* es heut' uns *letzen* mag. Wer guter Tat sich freut: ihm sei das *Mahl* erneut: der Labung darf er nah'n, die herste Gab' empfahn." Emphasis mine, to indicate the word-play on both "Mal/Mahl," and "letzt/letzen." "Mal" means "time;" "Mahl" means "supper." "Letzt" means 'last;" "letzen" means "refresh," or "feast." Thus while "zum letzten Male" means "for the last time," it simultaneously implies "to the Last Supper."

of my own sinful blood in mad flight must flow again into the world of thralldom to sin, pouring itself out in wild fear; once again it bursts open the gateway[61] through which it gushes now, here through the wound . . ."[62]

To distill these attributes a step further, we can summarize that the Grail is a blood-containing vessel, normally hidden from sight, but displayed at regular intervals to pour forth its contents. If we add to this picture the commonly recognized female/male genital symbolism of the Grail and holy spear in *Parsifal*, we have in the orbit of the Grail an unmistakable image of the female menstrual cycle.

Not the least remarkable aspect of this cycle is the operative taboo under which menstruation is ostensibly hidden from view, whereas its actual manifestations are in fact a most ordinary, and indeed generally quite visible, fact of everyday life. The taboo, nonetheless, renders the subject in effect perversely unmentionable.[63] In the 19th century, before the development of commercial sanitary pads, women's menstruation was a particularly visible phenomenon, manifested regularly in bloody rags, blood-

---

[61] The German is "Tor," a word-play on the central theme of foolishness.

[62] "Des Weihgefässes . . . heiligsten Blutes Quell' fühl' ich sie giessen in mein Herz; des eignen sündigen Blutes Gewell' in wahnsinniger Flucht muss mir zurück dann fliessen, in die Welt der Sündensucht mit wilder Scheu sich ergiessen; von neuem springt es das Tor, daraus es nun strömt hervor, hier durch die Wunde . . ."

[63] Otto Rank ties this taboo to the birth trauma. "Menstruation, which also 'periodically' continues the womb existence, seems to have been drawn into the general repression of the birth trauma by our civilization. Originally the sign of the woman's extremely desirable ability to become pregnant, it has become, with repression, the meeting-point of the most various neurotic disturbances." *The Trauma of Birth*, (New York, 1952, originally published 1924), p. 51, footnote #2.

stained clothing and bed-sheets, blood-infused bathwater,[64] and not uncommonly vestiges of blood along the floor.

This profound ambivalence is reflected in Mary Jane Lupton's observation that, "During the nineteenth and early twentieth centuries, women were both secretive and anxious about menstruation, swayed by a medical profession that tended to associate menstruation with pathology and to relate it to such disturbances as hysteria and madness."[65] Think of Kundry's mercurial outbursts. Again, Lupton writes, "As metaphor, menstruation is not a simple substitution of one word for another but rather a submerged signifier that is veiled or curtained. As veiled, menstruation necessitates oblique, covert metaphoric representation; as the unspoken, menstruation appears in disguise, resisting interpretation."[66]

The authors of a historical survey of undergarments write, "But how did women deal in daily life with monthly bleeding? As late as 1899, in a book on health for middle-class women written by a female physician, we find the admonition: 'It is highly distasteful to let the blood soak into one's chemise; indeed, wearing the same chemise 4-8 days carries with it danger of infection.' [H. B. Adams Lehmann, *Die Gesundheit im Haus*, (Stuttgart, 1899), p. 681.] This was a time-honored practice among rural women and women of the lower classes. Close-fitting dressings or sponges were in

[64] It was common for the same bathwater to be used by several people in a family, sequentially. See Mary Jane Lupton, *Menstruation and Psychoanalysis*, (University of Illinois Press, 1993), p. 50, & n. 32, p. 58.
[65] Mary Jane Lupton, *Menstruation and Psychoanalysis*, p. 66.
[66] *Ibid.*, p. 61.

use almost exclusively [by women] in theatrical professions, and very few women wore underpants or even used dressings fashioned from cloths or linen rags. Washing and changing of undergarments was regarded at that time as dangerous to health, fearing a blockage or an increased flow of bleeding."[67]

A graphic picture is painted succinctly by two historians of "the menstrual woman": "Most women seem to have accommodated [their periods] with self-sewn fabric pads, or, like rural women, to have eschewed padding or undergarments altogether. When they menstruated, they left behind them a trail of blood."[68]

Yet, as ordinary a phenomenon as the monthly bleeding of women (more or less half the population) was, the taboo cast a veil (albeit transparent—and we might add, hypocritical) over its ubiquitous presence. "Whereas the phallus is, in current psychoanalytic theory, the signifier of desire, menstrual blood is the undesired; as the phallus protrudes dominantly into space, menstruation hides in a closet—unspoken, reticent, veiled, ashamed to declare its difference. Menstruation is the gap in the text, the gaping wound concealed in the dream interpretation . . ."[69]

---

67 Almut Junker and Eva Stille, *Zur Geschichte der Unterwäsche 1700-1960*, (Historisches Museum Frankfurt, 1988), p. 336, my trans.
68 Sabine Hering and Gudrun Maierhof, *Die Unpäßliche Frau: Sozialgeschichte der Menstruation und Hygiene, 1860-1985*, (Pfaffenweiler, 1991), my trans.
This and the previous are quoted on the highly informative (and witty) website *The Museum of Menstruation & Women's Health*: www.mum.org.
69 Lupton, *op. cit.*, p. 61

We have seen (above) the almost violent linkage Amfortas draws in his monologue between his wound and the scarlet effusion emanating from the uncovered Grail. That ethereal essence flowing from the sacred vessel provokes a renewed and agonizing surge of bleeding from Amfortas's wound, "the wound that will never heal." In fantasy, it is commonplace—not only in the context of psychoanalysis—to regard the vagina as a wound. Karl Abraham, for instance, stresses that the menstrual flow of blood only serves to reinforce this basic fantasy: "The primary idea of the 'wound' is re-animated by the impression created by the first and each succeeding menstruation, and then once again by defloration; for both processes are connected with loss of blood and thus resemble an injury. . ."[70]

In Wolfram von Eschenbach's *Parzival*, Wagner's primary source, the wound of Anfortas is unambiguously to his genitals.

> One day, the king rode alone
> (to the sorrow of his near and dear)
> out on adventure:
> love would lead him to pleasure,
> for he was still much under love's sway.
> With a poisoned spear
> he was wounded in jousting
> (so that he never again would be well,
> your sweet uncle)

---

[70] Karl Abraham, "Manifestations of the Female Castration Complex," reprinted in *Selected Papers on Psychoanalysis*, trans., Douglas Bryan and Alix Strachey, (New York, 1971), p. 347. Quoted in Mary Jane Lupton, *Menstruation and Psychoanalysis*, pp. 132-3.

through his genitals.[71]

In *Parsifal,* Wagner transposes the locus of Amfortas's wound to his side, partly to parallel the wound in the side of the crucified Redeemer.[72] On the one hand, this transposition serves to mask somewhat the genital character of the wound, and hence its association with menstruation. On the other, the genital symbolism of the "wound in the side" (like the conventional and euphemistic "wound in the thigh," or "wound in the groin," so commonplace in medieval literature, and readily understood as such by its contemporaneous audience) remains clear enough, if for no other reason than that the wound was inflicted during (and as a result of) sexual congress with Kundry.

The medieval background of Amfortas's wound is summarized in *The Curse of Eve*:

> Most grail romances include the figure of the wounded king—the guardian of the grail, often called the Fisher King, is wounded in the thigh or between the two thighs. In all of the grail romances, this king has lost the use of his members and he cannot move without help. He will be healed only

---

[71] *Parzival,* 479, 3-12, my trans. "eins tages der künec al eine reit/(daz was gar den sînen leit)/ûz durch âventiure,/durch freude an minnen stiure:/des twanc in der minnen ger./Mit einem gelupten sper/Wart er ze tjostieren wunt,/sô daz er nimmer mêr gesunt/wart, der süeze œheim dîn,/durch die heidruose sîn."

[72] ". . . nun strömt [es] hervor, hier, durch die Wunde, der seinen gleich, geschlagen von desselben Speeres Streich, der dort dem Erlöser die Wunde stach . . . " " . . . now [it] gushes forth, here, through the wound, like His, struck by the same spear's stroke, that struck the wound in the Redeemer . . ."

when the good knight arrives and asks whom the grail serves. Although the grail king's wound is explicitly described as a genital wound only in Wolfram von Eschenbach's *Parzifal* the king's wound is always linked to sterility and to a general political and economic devastation that can only be repaired by the chaste knight's discovery of the grail secrets. And the sterility symbolized by the wound, along with the emphasis on sexual purity in grail romances, suggests that the grail king's wound might be seen as a sexual wound. This identification of the wound is further suggested in romances like Wolfram's, where the wound is identified as a punishment for a sexual transgression. In *Parzival,* the wound is a punishment for sexual promiscuity, and the grail king, Anfortas, is struck "through the scrotum"[73] with a wound that will not stop bleeding . . .

. . . The grail guardian's wound will not stop bleeding, and it bleeds from between the thighs. Whether or not the wound is a genital wound, the blood that continues to flow is similar to genital bleeding. But although genital bleeding is often considered a polluting blood . . . the grail guardian's bleeding wound does not identify his body as unworthy of access to holy relics. In fact, it does quite the opposite: the wound marks the body of the divinely ordained guardian of a holy relic. The

---

[73] Wolfram's word is "heidruose," denoting (not quite so specifically) "male genitals."

> wound that will not stop bleeding is represented as a purifying wound in the representation of]osephus in the *Estoire del saint graaL* That is, the wound in the thigh is called a punishment, but it is also an act of grace—it marks the body of God's chosen servant. In the *Estoire,* the blood of the wound is like sacrificial blood in that it purifies the sinful body that waits for the final healing and redemption that the good knight will bring.[74]

Though Amfortas implores his father, Titurel, to spare him the agonizing duty of presiding over the Grail rite, he is compelled to accede to his office. The Grail is uncovered, spreading its glow throughout the temple, and effecting the transubstantiation of the bread and wine on the feast table. The knights partake of the Eucharistic meal, as does Gurnemanz, who invites Parsifal to take a seat at the table with him and partake as well. Parsifal, however, stands aloof, transfixed. Only at the height of Amfortas's litany of pain has he clutched at his heart in empathetic participation in the Grail King's agony—anticipating the pivotal point of the entire work in Act II when, recoiling at Kundry's kiss, he will cry out, "Amfortas! The wound!"

The ritual concludes; the Grail is covered once more, returned to concealment in its reliquary, and is borne away by the Knights and Squires who file out of the temple, leaving Gurnemanz alone with the dazed Parsifal. "Why are

---

74 Peggy McCracken, *The Curse of Eve, the Wound of the Hero: Blood, Gender, and Medieval Literature,* (Univ. of Pennsylvania Press, 2003), pp. 99-100.

you still standing there?" he asks, visibly annoyed. "Do you know what you have seen?"[75] Receiving only a vague shake of the head in reply, exasperated, Gurnemanz says, "You are after all just a fool,"[76] pushing Parsifal rudely out into the wide world and onto his arduous path, apparently oblivious to the irony of the prophecy foretelling the Redeemer to be the very fool he is now brusquely showing the door. Lest the audience miss that point, Wagner has an ethereal voice intone what we have called the philosophical legend of the work, "Durch Mitleid wissend, der reine Tor . . ."

"Weißt du, was du sahst?" A profound question: perhaps the central question of this, Wagner's ultimate work. Parsifal has seen, has witnessed a shattering, blood-suffused, even elemental scene. What indeed are we to make of it?

Parsifal has witnessed a great mystery. Although puzzled as to its meaning, he is awe-struck by the inchoate sense of its gravity and significance. Thrust into the world by Gurnemanz, he embarks on a quest—not for Grail itself, as in the numerous medieval grail romances, but for the answer to this elemental question, "Weißt du, was du sahst?" His moment of enlightenment will come only in Kundry's embrace in the flower garden of Klingsor's castle in the next act. "Amfortas! The wound!" This empathetic experience proves to be the revelatory answer to Gurnemanz's question, and it is rooted in the sexual congress at whose brink Parsifal fatefully recoils, the lapse into intercourse that has laid low the Grail King, Amfortas.

---

[75] "Weißt du was du sahst?"
[76] "Du bist doch eben nur ein Tor!"

Knowledge is carnal knowledge.[77]

And the great mystery Parsifal has observed uncomprehending we now surmise is a sublimated manifestation of that putatively universal childhood experience to which Freud assigned the term "die Urszene," the "primal scene."[78] Otto Fenichel offers an illuminating descriptive phrase in his report of one analytic patient: "The observation of a primal scene . . . was thought of as the 'overwhelming unknown,'"[79] an epithet that aptly characterizes Parsifal's experience of the Grail ritual he has just been witness to.

> "The 'primal scene' is a scene of sexual intercourse between the parents and observed (or fantasized) by a child, who usually interprets it as an act of violent aggression on the part of the father. The memory of the primal scene feeds into most fantasies, and especially those of neurotics . . . The scene leads to the sexual arousal of the child, but at the same time induces castration anxiety and thus lays the foundation for the Oedipus complex. According to [Melanie] Klein, the child fantasizes that its parents are locked together in permanent intercourse; they merge to form the combined parent figure, and

[77] "And Adam knew Eve, his wife; and she conceived, and bare Cain . . ." *Genesis* 4:1. Luther's German verb is "erkannte;" the Latin Vulgate reads "cognovit."

[78] Sigmund Freud, letter to Wilhelm Fliess, May 2, 1897; "From the history of an infantile neurosis," (1918), reprinted in Peter Gay, *The Freud Reader* (London: Vintage, 1995).

[79] Otto Fenichel, *The Psychoanalytic Theory of Neurosis*, (Norton, NY, 1945), p. 483.

> torment and destroy one another in the act of copulation. The combined parent figure is one of the most terrifying fantasies of childhood . . . The scene is not understood by the child, remaining enigmatic but at the same time provoking sexual excitement."[80]

We should note that under the comparatively closer quarters prevailing in the typical living arrangements of the average poor or middle-class family in 19th century Europe, the child's actual witnessing of parental sex or hearing its provocative sounds through bedroom walls, was an eventuality more probable than it might seem to be today.

Klein stresses that in the child's imagination of the "combined parent" figure,[81] thus engaged in "permanent intercourse," it is not exclusively the mother who is the object of the aggression of the father; the father can also be fantasized as victim of mother's violence.[82] In *Parsifal,* accordingly, it is Amfortas who is grievously wounded in the sexual act. Fenichel generalizes: "what is always present [in the experience of the primal scene] is the linking together of the conceptions 'sexual satisfaction' and 'danger' . . ."[83] And the "danger" perceived is invariably genital. In this light, we can see that Amfortas's wound is as emblematic of the castration threat as the more overtly genital wound of his medieval model, Parzifal. This threat is central to the

---

[80] This summary of the psychoanalytic term is taken from the *Wikipedia* entry for "primal scene."

[81] Cf., Shakespeare, *Othello,* (I, 1, 126-7), "The beast with two backs."

[82] Klein, Melanie. *Narrative of a child analysis. The conduct of the psychoanalysis of children as seen in the treatment of a ten-year-old boy,* (New York: Basic Books,1961), pp. 122, 196.

[83] Fenichel, *op. cit.,* p. 214.

Oedipus Complex, as well as to the common fantasy of the vagina as the locus of danger—be it the *"vagina dentata"* imagined as a devouring mouth armed with teeth, or the menstrually bleeding vagina.

On the positive side of the ledger, Freud noted the effect of the primal scene on the development of intellectual curiosity.[84] This relates of course to Parsifal's arduous quest for the answer to Gurnemanz's question, "Weißt du was du sahst?" In a useful overview of the psychoanalytic literature on the primal scene, Knafo and Feiner note that such curiosity is based on "the easily observable interest children have in their parents' relationship. Furthermore, curiosity is an essential component of ambitious strivings . . ."[85] In this sense, the primal scene—"what Parsifal saw"—appears not only as the source and foundation of anxiety, but as the impetus setting him on his quest for enlightenment.

[84] Sigmund Freud, "Some psychical consequences of the anatomical distinction between the sexes," *Standard Edition*, James Strachey, ed., v. XIX, (London, Hogarth Press, 1961), pp. 248-58.
[85] Danielle Knafo & Kenneth Feiner, *Unconscious Fantasies and the Relational World*, (New York, London, 2013), p. 41.

III: Klingsor's Garden:

The Language of Flowers

"Die Zeit is da!"[86] declares Klingsor, gloating over Parsifal's fateful approach to the enchanted castle and magic garden. And moments later, "Once again in thrall to my spell at the right time."[87] In the preceding chapter, we noted Kundry's verbal anticipation of this pronouncement in Act I, as well as Amfortas's closely related "Die Stunde nah't,"[88] and Gurnemanz's "Die Stund' ist da"[89] announcing the recurrence of the Grail ritual in Act III.

These statements are to be considered on two levels. First, they echo Jesus's words, repeated several times, in closely related terms, regarding the imminent time of his crucifixion. In Luther's German, "Gehet hin in die Stadt zu einem und sprecht zu ihm: Der Meister läßt dir sagen: Meine Zeit ist nahe,[90] ich will bei dir Ostern halten mit meinen Jüngern." (Matt. 26: 18) In Luther's *John*: "Meine Stunde is noch nicht gekommen." (*John* 2: 4) And also: "Meine Zeit ist noch nicht hier . . ." (*John* 7: 6) These echoes

---

[86] "The time has come!" literally, "The time is here!"
[87] "Meinem Banne wieder verfallen heut' zur rechten Zeit."
[88] "The hour draws near."
[89] "The hour has come."
[90] Intriguing to note is that the modern "Einheitsübersetzung" reads "meine Zeit ist da."

reverberate with the scriptural theme of sacrifice running through *Parsifal* on the conscious level.

On a subliminal level, "time" and "the hour" establish a theme of recurrence and arrival, like a clock methodically striking the stations of the day—"day after day,"[91] as the Grail Knights chant, recounting their regularly recurring task of preparation of the Eucharistic meal. Looking ahead to Act III, even more evocative of the association of the Grail ritual to clock work is the tolling of the bells heard above the Knights' repetitive chant "zum Letzten Male,"[92] adjuring the recalcitrant Amfortas to carry out his office and uncover the Grail.

On account of their regularity, their periodicity, Freud interpreted clocks as symbolizing the female reproductive apparatus. ". . . The clock is the symbol of the female genital. The clock . . . receives this role of the genital organ through its relation to periodic occurrences at equal intervals. A woman may for instance be found to boast that her menstruation is as regular as clockwork . . . The ticking of the clock may be compared to the throbbing of the clitoris during sexual excitement . . . Flowerpots and vases are, as are all vessels, also female symbols."[93] This latter interpretation conforms to the symbolism of the Grail we have already noted, of course. But the veiled symbolism of

---

[91] "Tag für Tag."

[92] "for the last time"

[93] Sigmund Freud, "The Sense of Symptoms." In James Strachey, *The Standard Edition of the Complete Psychological Works of Sigmund Freud* (London: Hogarth Press), Vol. 16, pp. 264-269. Also in *A General Introduction to Psychoanalysis,* Part 3, XVII, "The Meaning of the Symptoms," (1920).

clockworks pertains most directly to the menstrual theme explored in relation to the Grail rite of Act I.

More pointedly, Act II will be acted out in Klingsor's magic garden of flowers, in which the flowers metamorphose (we're tempted to say transubstantiate) into seductive women intent on ensnaring the virginal hero on Klingsor's nefarious command. Kundry is a flower too, a "rose of hell"[94] Klingsor dubs her. In fact, she is Klingsor's principal flower. Of flowers, Freud wrote unambiguously, "Blossoms and flowers represent the female genitals . . . Do not forget that the blossoms are really the genitals of the plants."[95] We are reminded also of the imagery of the "garden enclosed" from the *Song of Solomon*:

> My sister, beloved spouse, you are a garden enclosed, a spring enclosed,
> a fountain sealed. . .
> A garden fountain, a fount of living waters that flow from Lebanon.[96]

At once, Klingsor turns to conjure up Kundry from the "death sleep" in which he keeps her, as it were in deep freeze, until he requires her services. He knows the secret of

---

[94] "Höllenrose"

[95] Sigmund Freud, *A General Introduction to Psychoanalysis*, Part 2, X, "Symbolism in the Dream," (1920).

[96] My translation of Luther's text, which Wagner knew and revered: "Meine Schwester, liebe Braut, du bist ein verschlossener Garten, eine verschlossene Quelle, ein versiegelter Born . . . Ein Gartenbrunnen bist du, ein Born lebendiger Wasser, die vom Libanon fließen." *Song of Solomon* 4: 12-15.

releasing her from the grip of his curse.[97] Underlying the fiction of Klingsor's master/slave relation to Kundry is the fantasy of necrophilia, explored in depth with respect to *The Ring of the Nibelung* in *The Wagner Complex*.[98] Sandor Ferenczi summarizes the essential nature of the necrophiliac fantasy:

> Many neurotics unconsciously regard coitus as an activity which, either directly or subsequently, is calculated to injure life or limb, and in particular to damage the genital organ, i.e., an act in which are combined gratification and severe anxiety. Murder then at any rate partly sub-serves the purpose of avoiding anxiety by rendering the love-object incapable of inflicting injury; gratification can then be enjoyed undisturbed by castration anxiety. In these phantasies of aggression the woman is attacked in the first instance with external weapons (knife, dagger, or, in the case of throttling, with parts of the body which are not usually protected, i.e., the hand), following on which coitus is performed, that is to say, the penis is employed as weapon against a now harmless object."[99]

Ferenczi associates neurotic anxiety over coitus with the common fantasy of the *vagina dentata*, the vagina as a

[97] "Im Todesschlafe hält der Fluch sie fest, der ich den Krampf zu lösen weiß.—Auf denn! Ans Werk!"

[98] Tom Artin, *The Wagner Complex*, (Free Scholar Press, 2012 & 2015), pp. 156, ff. In that book, I cite in passing the necrophiliac fantasy underlying this relation in *Parsifal*, pp. 169-70.

[99] Sandor Ferenczi, "On Unconscious Phantasies of Sexual Lust-Murder," section 3 of "Psychoanalysis of Sexual Habits," in *Selected Papers of Sandor Ferenczi: Further Contributions to the Theory and Technique of Psychoanalysis*, vol. II (New York, 1952), p. 279.

devouring mouth armed with teeth.

In her case history of an analytic patient for whom this fantasy was primary, H. Segal describes his rationale. "[He] started extolling the virtues of a corpse as a sexual object. He described with relish the feeling of power and security that he could enjoy in making love to a corpse: it is there when wanted, you put it away when finished with it, it makes no demands, it is never frustrating, never unfaithful, never reproachful; persecution and guilt, he said, could be quite done away with."[100]

In this light, we appreciate the trenchancy of Kundry's taunt, "Are you chaste?" On one hand, we cannot psychoanalyze Klingsor, not only because we cannot put him on the analytic couch to elicit his associations, but more fundamentally because he has no psyche to analyze; he consists of nothing more than the words Wagner committed to his pages. We can surmise, however, that underlying the

---

[100] H. Segal, "A Necrophiliac Phantasy," *International Journal of Psychoanalysis*, vol. 34 (London, 1953), pp. 98-101. Necrophilia gives the appearance of a tabooed subject, since it is barely touched in the psychoanalytic literature. Among the few items the bibliography comprises, most suggestive by far is Segal's paper, which while restricting itself to a single case history, and a fragmentary one at that, nevertheless outlines a general interpretation of the perversion. Ferenczi's contribution cited above adds an important theoretical dimension to Segal's clinical observations. Aside from these brief discussions, deserving mention are Ernest Jones, *On the Nightmare* (New York, 1951), which contains several pertinent comments, and Klaf and Brown, "Necrophilia, Brief Review and Case Report," *Psychiatric Quarterly*, vol. 32 (Utica, 1958), pp. 645-652. Although the reason for this psychoanalytic neglect may be that as an actual perversion necrophilia is encountered only infrequently in clinical practice, Segal's paper implies its prevalence as a theme in fantasy—which is our interest here.

idea of Klingsor's intense need to subdue his sexual impulses[101] and thus gain acceptance among the Grail Knighthood, a need so great as to prompt self-castration, is the kind of debilitating anxiety over coitus Ferenczi and Segal observe in their neurotic patients. Klingsor is "chaste," not because he has learned to control his impulses, but only because, having violently cut away the offending organ from his own body, he is immune to Kundry's allure.

Klingsor watches now from the battlements as Parsifal encounters the sorcerer's chattel knights, in thrall to him as a result of their own lapses into the arms of the lovely flower maidens. Parsifal subdues each in pointedly bloody battle, in continuation of the blood motif that serves here as fitting prelude to the main, pivotal action of Act II in the magic flower garden. Klingsor notes the "roses" in Parsifal's cheek as, astonished, the young hero espies the garden, another foreshadowing of the abundant flower imagery to come.[102]

The flower maidens bemoan their overmastered lovers, but only until Parsifal enters the garden and parries their reproaches. "You beautiful girls, was I not obliged to strike them? After all, to you, lovelies, they barred my way."

"You were coming to us?" the first fickle flower asks him.

Her counterpart: "Had you seen us already?"[103]

---

[101] "Furchtbare Not! Ungebändigten Sehnens Pein, schrecklichster Triebe Höllendrang . . ."

[102] "Wie lachen ihm die Rosen der Wangen, da kindisch erstaunt in den einsamen Garten er blickt!"

[103] "Sahst du uns schon?" a curious echo of Siegfried's astonished question put to Hagen, "Du riefst mich Siegfried: sahst du mich schon?"

Parsifal's flirtatious blandishments now convert the initially hostile flower maidens into fawning rivals for his attention.

"Who now will play with us?" the flower maidens pout in unison.

"I'll gladly do that!" Parsifal replies.

It must be said that, given the austerity of the Grail ritual Parsifal has been witness to, the depths to which he has appeared to have been shaken by it, the sobering severity of his summary dismissal by Gurnemanz onto an arduous path of spiritual trial and quest, his frivolous and flirtatious behavior with the flower maidens now seems perhaps out of character—our hero's innocence and ostensible "foolishness" notwithstanding. We may be forgiven, though, if, swept up in the rapturous beauty of Wagner's score, and the compelling architecture of his narrative, we are inclined to concede poetic license on this point—call it "willing suspension of disbelief," or simply enthusiastic indulgence.

In the light of our reading of the blood imagery in Act I, Mary Jane Lupton's observation that, "the menstrual signification of flowers is widespread—a familiar emblem in mythology, a symbol in dreams and poetry,"[104] is intriguing, although evidence for its direct pertinence to *Parsifal* is probably scant.[105] What is obvious, though, is that the gist of

---

Götterdämmerung, Act I, scene 2. I take it this is a verbal coincidence without greater significance.

[104] Lupton, *Menstruation and Psychoanalysis*, p. 62.

[105] A textual hint (admittedly tenuous) in this direction is Klingsor's odd designation of the death-sleep coma he keeps Kundry in as ". . . den

Freud's general interpretation of flowers as symbolizing the female genitals is totally apt, even on the overt level of Wagner's story. Klingsor's "flowers" metamorphose into alluring women whose explicit purpose is the seduction of Grail Knights he hopes to ensnare. Whether or not the magic flower garden is imbued with menstrual overtones, it is clearly conceived—consciously—as emblematic of the seductive powers of the female genital apparatus.

Easily missed amid the spectacle of the magic garden and its gaily floral denizens, the score's lilting, bouncy music throughout this episode, and especially because these words are sung by groups in unison and thus difficult to make out in performance, the flower maidens echo (with light-hearted irony on Wagner's part[106]) the prophecy of the Redeemer to come: "der reine Tor, harre sein den ich erkor." Chorus I sings "Auf! Weichet dem Toren!"[107] Chorus II responds, "Doch sei er uns erkoren!"[108] The operative words are the rhyming "Toren" and "erkoren." Suddenly regaining his composure, Parsifal rejects the flower maidens altogether. "Desist! You won't catch me!" he says. The musical setting of his rebuff also takes a sudden turn from frivolous to sternly serious.

And now, above the extended chord the orchestra has begun

Krampf [den ich] zu lösen weiß," " . . . the cramp I know how to ease." "Krampf" is not an obvious word to denote "coma," or even "curse" ("Fluch"), and it is suggestive of the menstrual idiom "cramps," in German, "Menstrualkrämpfe."

[106] On the comedic side of the Wagnerian character, see Joachim Köhler, *The Laughing Wagner*, (Free Scholar Press, 2015).

[107] "Away! Shun the fool!"

[108] "Then let him be chosen for us!"

under Parsifal's final word, "nicht," and on the same note, an octave higher, comes what is surely the most electrifying moment of this entire "*Bühnenweihfestspiel*"[109] as Kundry calls out to him, "Parsifal!—Weile!" Parsifal's "nicht" dissolving into Kundry's "Parsifal" as though their two bodies were already merging into one. It is an effect so arresting and erotic we understand at once that the action has risen to an altogether more serious level than the frivolous flirtations of the flower maidens.

"Parsifal" is the name he could not recall in response to Gurnemanz's questioning. At its sound on Kundry's lips he muses, "Dreaming once, my mother called me that." This revelation of his name is merely a prelude to the pivotal, shattering insight he will experience in Kundry's kiss. Her appearance here marks the beginning of the barely veiled Oedipal theme of this work. If in Act I Kundry has served as Herzeleide's ambassador, now in Act II she becomes quite overtly Parsifal's mother-surrogate—the object of Oedipal fantasy.

Kundry dismisses the frivolous flower maidens. "He was not summoned [here] to play with you,"[110] she chides. The flower maidens withdraw, reluctantly, pouting over their loss. "Farewell, farewell! Farewell you fair one, you proud one, you . . . fool!"[111] And, delighted with this parting joke (charged with meaning they cannot appreciate), the maidens depart in a flurry of girlish giggling, leaving Kundry and Parsifal to their much more pregnant affair.

---

[109] "Stage consecrating festival play."
[110] ". . . nicht euch ward er zum Spiele bestellt . . ."
[111] "Leb wohl, du Holder, du Stolzer, du . . . Tor!"

"Did you call me [who is] nameless?" asks Parsifal.

Kundry tells him ("foolish pure one"[112]) that she named him "Fal parsi," an anagram of "Parsifal," a name whose dubious Arabic etymology Wagner had derived from Joseph Görres's Introduction to his edition of Lohengrin.[113] When he explained the name's origin to Judith Gautier, she "pointed out that *fal parsi* did not occur in Arabic, but Wagner brushed her objection aside. Görres probably had no Arabic, he wrote back, and must have heard it from an Orientalist. 'Besides, that doesn't matter either. I don't care what the Arabic words really mean, and I very much doubt if there will be many Orientalists among my future audiences!"[114] Wagner's cavalier response to Gautier's scrupulous critique actually veils a serious artistic stance central to our current analysis. The underlying or informing meaning of a work of art must trump mere outward fidelity to narrative sources.

In her next few lines, Kundry tells him first that she named him "Fal Parsi," and then that his father Gamuret, with his dying breath "in Arabian lands," called him, unborn in his mother's womb, by the name "Parsifal." She has waited here for Parsifal to inform him of this, and asks rhetorically, "what drew you here if not the wish for the knowledge?"[115]

Parsifal replies, "I never saw, never dreamed, what now I see, and what fills me with dread." This declaration encapsulates the inchoate experience of the child witnessing

---

[112] " . . . tör'ger Reiner . . ."

[113] Joseph Görres, Einleitung: "Über den Dichtungskreis des heiligen Grales," *Lohengrin, ein altteutsches Gedicht,* (Heidelberg, 1813), p. VI.

[114] Gregor-Dellin, op. cit., p. 447.

[115] " . . . was zog dich her, wenn nicht der Kunde Wunsch?"

(or merely fantasizing) the primal scene. And whereas the primal scene was adumbrated in highly symbolic form in the Grail ritual of Act I, here in Act II—as we shall shortly see—it is actualized.

Kundry, too, has seen things. She tells Parsifal: "I came from far away, where I saw much. I saw the child at his mother's breast; his earliest babbling still laughs in my ear."[116] Wagner's verb is "ersah," which has to be rendered in English as "saw," although the German word connotes more. "Ersehen" (distinct from "sehen") implies "understanding," or "gaining insight into," or "perceiving." Kundry has not merely *seen*, but in seeing has as it were penetrated mysteries. She thus extends and deepens the theme of seeing, whose affective undercurrent is witnessing of the primal scene.

Consider the sensual tenor of Kundry's description of Herzeleide's relation to her infant son: "Bedded down gently on soft moss, whom sweetly she lulled to sleep with caresses, over whose slumber the mother's longing—[though] fearful with care—stood guard, who was awakened in the morning by the hot dew of mother's tears."[117] The erotically freighted words in this passage are, "Kosen," "Sehnen," and "heiße Tau [der Muttertränen]," not to mention the initial "gebettet." Taken individually, none, perhaps, would arouse our attention, but collectively, indeed

---

[116] "Von weit her kam ich, wo ich viel ersah: Ich sah das Kind an seiner Mutter Brust, sein erstes Lallen lacht mir noch im Ohr . . . "

[117] "Gebettet sanft auf weichen Moosen, den hold geschläfert sie mit Kosen, dem, bang in Sorgen, den Schlummer bewacht' der Mutter Sehnen, den weckt' am Morgen der heiße Tau der Muttertränen."

compacted into a single sentence, they charge Kundry's narrative with erotic valence in keeping with the overall drift of the action whose affect is Oedipal longing, and whose goal is Parsifal's seduction.

Kundry recounts how Herzeleide, still mourning her husband Gamuret's death in knightly combat, had determined to save Parsifal from a similar fate by retiring far into the forest, living cut off from courtly and martial society. Here, plainly, is the theme—listed at the outset of our argument—of maternal sacrifice. We recall Freud's identification of "the motif . . . of the mother who introduces the son to sexual intercourse sacrificing her own person in order to rescue him from the dangers of masturbation, which to the child appear hugely life-threatening."[118]

"Oh! What pleasure and laughter when she then, searching, [finally] found [literally, overtook] you; when then her arm embraced you passionately, did you not then even fear her kisses?"[119] Parsifal had strayed ever further and for longer periods from his mother's home, Kundry relates, until finally he abandoned her altogether. "She waited[120] [through] nights and days, until her laments fell silent, her grief gnawed at her pain, she pleaded for quiet death, the sorrow broke her heart, and . . . Herzeleide . . . died."[121]

---

118 Sigmund Freud to Stefan Zweig, September 4, 1936, citation above.

119 "Hei! Was ihr das Lust und Lachen schuf, wann sie suchend dann dich ereilt; wann dann ihr Arm dich wütend umschlang, ward dir es wohl gar beim Küssen bang?"

120 The verb is "harrte," as in the prophecy: "Harre sein den ich erkor."

121 "Sie harrte Nächt und Tage, bis ihr verstummt' die Klage, der Gram ihr zehrte den Schmerz, um stillen Tod sie warb: ihr brach das Leid das Herz, und—Herzeleide—starb."

Recall Freud's pointed formulation of maternal sacrifice: "durch Preisgabe ihrer eigenen Person."

Hearing Kundry's story, Parsifal berates himself: "Woe! Woe! What have I done? Where was I? Mother! Sweet, gracious mother! Your son, your son had to murder you! Oh fool! Stupid, staggering fool. Where were you straying about, forgetting her—forgetting yourself, yourself? Beloved, most precious mother!"

The sophistry of Kundry's reply insinuates her physical caresses. "Confession will end guilt in remorse; knowledge will turn foolishness into sense. Come to know the love that embraced Gamuret, when the flames of Herzeleide's passion flooded burning over him!"[122] Once again, Freud's "Ur-motif": " . . . the mother who introduces the son to sexual intercourse . . . " Kundry, mother's messenger, mother's surrogate, now merges her identity fully with Herzeleide's: "She who once lent you life and limb, whom death and foolishness must yield to, she offers you today, as mother's blessing's final greeting, love's first kiss."[123]

The *merger* of Kundry and Herzeleide can also be thought of (paradoxically) as *splitting*. Without venturing too far into the thickets of object relations theory, we can say that Herzeleide represents the self-sacrificing aspect of "mother," while Kundry represents the seductive, "exciting" aspect,

---

122 "Bekenntnis wird Schuld in Reue enden; Erkenntnis in Sinn die Torheit wenden. Die Liebe lerne kennen, die Gamuret umschloß, als Herzeleids Entbrennen ihn sengend überfloß!"

123 "Die Leib und Leben einst dir gegeben, der Tod und Torheit weichen muß, sie beut dir heut', als Muttersegens letzten Gruß, der Liebe—ersten Kuß."

initiating the son into the mysteries of sex. Bending over Parsifal, Kundry kisses him long and passionately "on his mouth" (as Wagner's stage directions stipulate). Kundry is Herzeleide; Parsifal, Gamuret. Thus is the primal scene not merely witnessed or fantasized, but enacted in the flesh. We could say, paradoxically, it is simultaneously enacted and reenacted.

Kundry and Parsifal remain locked in a long embrace, during which the music is at first ruminative, then increasingly agitated. Parsifal starts up, clutching his heart, and cries suddenly, "Amfortas! The wound! The wound! It burns here in my side!" In sexual congress with Kundry (just short of penetration), Parsifal has had an epiphany to be sure, although its exact nature merits closer scrutiny.

It is not obvious, for instance, why his arousal and embrace with Kundry should put Parsifal in mind of the wound in Amfortas's side. Presumably the actual threat to Parsifal, lying vulnerable in Kundry's arms, would be from Klingsor, wielding the holy spear, as when he inflicted the wound on Amfortas. But Klingsor is nowhere in evidence at this point. He reappears only near the end of the Act.

What in Kundry's embrace, then, would put Parsifal in mind of the wound? The fantasy of the vagina as wound is commonplace, whether derived from the idea that the lack of a penis implies castration, or from the sight of menstrual blood. We have cited several variations on this fantasy. As noted, Wagner's immediate source, Wolfram's *Parzifal*, identifies Anfortas's wound explicitly as genital. We saw also that the child typically interprets the primal scene as a violent interaction between parents, resulting in injury to one or both.

"I saw the wound bleeding," cries Parsifal. "Now it bleeds in me! Here! Here!" But he abruptly shifts from the vision of a bleeding wound to the sensation of desire burning in his heart. "No! No! It is not the wound. Let its blood flow away! Here! Here! in my heart, the blaze! The desire, the terrible desire that seizes and masters all my senses! Oh, agony of love!" In one sense, we have here a heightened version of the struggle that tears Tannhäuser apart between lust for Venus and chaste longing for Elisabeth.

More important, the shift from bleeding wound to *searing pain in the heart* is tantamount to a shift of focus from Amfortas (male) to Herzeleide (female). "Herz" (heart) and "Leid" (injury, wrong, harm, hurt). This is not so much a shift *from* male to female as an inclusion of female with male, like the combined parent concept, alluded to above, or more generally the concept of the androgyne, to which we shall return in due course.[124]

It is also a sublimation, a displacement upwards from the genitals to the higher, less erotically freighted and tabooed regions of the body. Parsifal's abrupt shift from wound to burning heart is really a form of denial. Where, after all, is

---

[124] On the theme of androgyny in Wagner generally, see Jean-Jacques Nattiez, *Wagner Androgyne*, (Princeton, 1993). Given his overarching theme, Nattiez is counter-intuitively dismissive of psychoanalytic literary exegesis on the grounds that it legitimizes overly permissive interpretation.

References to other recent studies on this aspect (androgyny) can be found in William Kinderman, "The Challenge of Wagner's Parsifal," in *A Companion to Wagner's Parsifal*, (Camden House, 2005), p.24, footnote 56.

the "burning passion" of erotic arousal felt? Not in the heart, to be sure, but in the genitals. If we say we do feel the passion of love in the heart (or what seems to be the heart), nevertheless it cannot be said that what Parsifal feels for Kundry is love in any meaningful sense of the word. Her seduction is overtly and exclusively sexual, with the aim of ensnaring Parsifal in service to the sorcerer Klingsor—there is no question of involvement of the "heart" in this affair. Parsifal says as much when he describes what he is feeling: "How everything shudders, quakes, and twitches in sinful craving!"[125]

Now there is a second, sudden shift in his monologue. According to Wagner's stage direction, Parsifal "falls into a complete rapture."[126] The last word might also be translated as "trance." He is lost in a vision of the Grail—the "vessel of salvation," as he calls it—in which "the holy blood begins to glow. Bliss of redemption, divinely mild, trembles far and wide in every soul. Only here, in my heart, will the agony not ease."

But what has Parsifal done? Why is he uniquely guilty, and of what? On the contrary, he has just drawn back from the brink of sin (if intercourse be sin) with Kundry.

"I hear the Saviour's lament, the lament, oh! the lament over the desecration of the temple: 'Redeem, rescue me from sin-stained hands!'"[127] The penultimate word here is

---

125 "Wie alles schauert, bebt, und zuckt in sündigem Verlangen!"

126 ". . . gerät . . . in völlige Entrücktheit."

127 "Des Heilands Klage da vernehm' ich, die Klage, ach! die Klage um das entweihte Heiligtum: 'Erlöse, rette mich aus schuldbefleckten Händen!'"

"schuldbefleckt," which does indeed mean, as I have translated it, "sin-stained." But, especially in its context here modifying the noun "hands," the word resonates with the connotation of the similar word "selbstbefleckung," the standard 19th century euphemism for masturbation.

We recall Freud's analysis in the altogether different context of his letter to Zweig of the novella the writer had sent him[128]: " . . . the emphasis on the hands and their activity achieved with such uncanny mastery by you is downright revelatory. In masturbation, after all, the hands effect their genital function. In your novella, the young player's role as son is indicated so unmistakably that it is hard to believe you had not pursued a conscious intention. I know, however, that this was not the case, and that you allowed your unconscious to be at work." Parsifal's combination of "sin-stained hands" and "the Saviour's" plea to be "rescued," is consistent with Freud's "Ur-motif" of the mother who *rescues* her son from the dangers of masturbation through self-sacrifice. We may also infer that like Zweig, Wagner would have been guided by his unconscious, so that these themes (or "Ur-motifs") inform his work independent of conscious intentions. This interpretation is reinforced by the conclusion of Parsifal's monologue: "And I—the fool, the coward, fled off to wild boyish deeds."[129] In German, the word is "Knabentaten," hinting at the boyish habit (Freud called it the "primal addiction"[130]) of masturbation. Dropping to his knees, he

[128] *Vierundzwanzig Stunden aus dem Leben einer Frau* (*Twenty-four Hours in the Life of Woman*).
[129] "Und ich—der Tor, der Feige, zu wilde Knabentaten floh ich hin!"
[130] Sigmund Freud, letter to Fliess, Dec. 22, 1897

cries, "Redeemer! Saviour! Lord of grace! How may I—sinner—atone for my sin?"

Kundry tries to snap him out of his trance state: "Promised Hero! Flee the delusion!" But Parsifal, still kneeling, vividly depicts Amfortas's seduction. "Yes! This voice! This is how she called him; and this look, I recognize it clearly—and this, that laughed at him so illicitly; the lips—yes—this is how they quivered for him, this is how her neck bent down—this is how she lifted her head boldly—this is how laughingly her curls fluttered—just so her arm twined about his neck—just so her cheek fawned softly! Leagued with all torments of pain, she kissed away from him salvation of [his] soul.! Ha! This kiss!"

With his fantasy of the seduction of Amfortas—subsumed under the fiction's rubric of "compassion"—Parsifal graphically projects the primal scene, only marginally displaced in that Kundry and Amfortas are stand-ins for Herzeleide and Gamuret. Kundry for that matter has so closely identified herself with Parsifal's mother as to have merged functionally with her in any case.

We noted in the previous chapter that Amfortas's wound, like the wound of the Grail King in all the medieval sources, is a marginally displaced genital wound, and hence represents castration fear. Now we are in a position to pierce to the heart of the mystery of *Parsifal*, the idea of redemption at its core. On the story's surface, the primal sin that menaces the Grail Knighthood, and for which Amfortas has suffered his debilitating wound—the sin from whose brink Parsifal has stepped back just at the last, redeeming instant—is sexual intercourse. Redemption from the stain, the curse of this sin lies in chastity. Parsifal sets off on his road to redemption when he recoils from Kundry's fatal kiss, and rejects her attempt at seduction—though the temptation was great and has shaken him to his core. We noted the bitter irony of Kundry's taunt to Klingsor, "Bist du keusch?" ("Are you chaste?") We know that Klingsor is "chaste" only because he has inflicted on himself the punishment adumbrated in Amfortas's symbolic wound: castration. Parsifal and those Grail Knights who have not succumbed to Kundry's charms, or to the flower maidens', find redemption in chastity, lived out in mastery of, in defiance of the lusts of the flesh.

But what sense does this actually make? Is intercourse *per se* really a sin? Is chastity truly a viable or desirable way of life in the context of 19th century bourgeois German society? Does the renunciation of sex constitute the essence of virtue in the real world?[131] This dichotomy and its attendant

---

[131] A psychoanalytic description of instinctual renunciation is given at the online site *No Subject – Encyclopedia of Lacanian Psychoanalysis*: "When the Id makes an instinctual demand of an erotic or aggressive nature on a human being, the most simple and natural response for the ego, which governs the apparatus for thinking and muscle innervation, is to satisfy this by an action. This satisfaction of the instinct is felt as pleasure by the Ego, just as not satisfying this instinct would undoubtedly become a source of discomfort. Now, it may happen that the Ego eschews satisfaction of the instinct because of external obstacles—namely, when it realizes that the action in question would bring in its course serious danger to the Ego. Such a refraining from satisfaction, an 'instinctual renunciation' because of external obstacles—as we say, in obedience to the reality-principle—is never pleasurable. The instinctual renunciation would bring about a lasting painful tension if we did not succeed in diminishing the strength of the instinctual urge itself through a displacement of energy. This instinctual renunciation may also be forced

dilemma are essentially the same as those at the heart of *Tannhäuser*, as well as of countless artistic works of Western civilization. Nonetheless, Wagner, the sensualist, never behaved as though he subscribed to such desiccated moralism in real life, Cosima's overbearing frigidity notwithstanding. It is significant that in *Parsifal* sexuality is entirely dissociated from procreation, and even from love. It figures as an autonomous and perilous drive, doubtless related to Schopenhauer's unconscious "will."

We can make sense of *Parsifal* only if we regard it as an allegory, or, to use the Freudian term, a sublimation. Quite overtly in *Parsifal*, the consequence of sexual intercourse is the threat of castration—the genital wound inflicted by Klingsor with the holy (or more pointedly, phallic) spear. This is precisely the anxiety at the heart of the child's experience of the primal scene, the emotional and ontogenetic motif informing this *"Bühnenweihfestspiel."* Witnessing (or fantasizing) parental sex is first of all an exclusionary experience: the parent couple is engaged in a private act from which the child is excluded, which it can only observe voyeuristically. But the vicarious experience is exciting, and prompts identification with one or both

---

on us, however, by other motives, which we rightly call inner ones. In the course of individual development a part of the inhibiting forces in the outer world becomes internalized; a standard is created in the Ego which opposes the other faculties by observation, criticism, and prohibition. We call this new standard the Super-ego . . . While, however, instinctual renunciation for external reasons is only painful, renunciation for internal reasons, in obedience to the demands of the Super-ego, has another economic effect. It brings besides the inevitable pain a gain in pleasure to the Ego—as it were, a substitutive satisfaction." http://nosubject.com/index.php?title=Renunciation.

parents. Typically, the experience provokes an Oedipal response—in the male child, the wish to assume the position of the father, i.e., to have intercourse with his mother. This wish, in turn, triggers the fear of castration, meted out in fantasy by an avenging father.

To evade this catastrophe, Parsifal pushes Kundry away: "Corrupter! Depart from me! Forever—forever—from me!"[132] This injunction is puzzling, not only because Kundry will in fact reappear prominently in Act III as a penitent, and receive baptism and redemption by Parsifal's own hand, but more immediately because shortly, Act II will conclude with Parsifal's enigmatic parting address to Kundry: "You know where you can find me!"[133] (Indeed, in the following chapter, we will see that Parsifal and Kundry actually—if paradoxically—merge into a single identity.)

Kundry reproaches Parsifal for his coldness, and persevering in her wheedling sophistry argues that just as he is compassionate with others, he should extend his compassion to her as well. "Be you [a] redeemer, what stops you, [you] bad man, from uniting with me for my salvation?"[134] An odd rationale, certainly. But Kundry is nothing if not mercurial. " . . . Let me . . . unite with you for just one hour, and, though God and the world cast me out, be cleansed of sin and redeemed in you!"[135]

---

[132] "Verderberin! Weiche von mir! Ewig—ewig—von mir!"
[133] "Du weißt—wo du mich wieder finden kanst!"
[134] "Bist du Erlöser, was bannt dich, Böser, nicht mir auch zum Heil dich zu einen?"
[135] " . . . laß mich . . . nur eine Stunde mich dir vereinen, und, ob mich Gott und Welt verstößt, in dir entsündigt sein und erlöst!"

"You would be damned with me for eternity for [the sake of] one hour's forgetting of my mission in your arms' embrace," Parsifal counters. "You too am I sent to save, if you will turn away forever from your desires." He continues, using the metaphor of a "source," in the sense of "fountain," or "spring," a feminine metaphor reminiscent of the menstrual imagery of Act I. "The draught ["Labung"] that ends your suffering is not offered by the fountain from which it [i.e., Kundry's suffering] flows: salvation will never be given you until that fountain is shut off for you. It is a different one—a different one, ah! for which I saw the brotherhood yonder, lamenting and languishing in terrible distress, tormenting and mortifying their flesh. But who recognizes it, clear and bright, the only true fountain of salvation? Oh misery, flight from all rescue! Oh, worldly mad illusion: thirsting for salvation, to long for the fountain of perdition!"

"So was it my kiss that made you clear-eyed about the world?, then my total love-embrace will bring you to divinity." Kundry's words are virtually a paraphrase of the serpent's seductive words to Eve. "Redeem the world, if that be your office: if that hour made you a god, for its sake let me be damned eternally, my wound never heal!" What Kundry's "wound" is remains unclear. In his notes to *Parsifal: A New English Translation With Commentary*, Derrick Everett suggests that "It is difficult to see Kundry's reference to her own wound . . . as anything other than sexual metaphor."[136] This interpretive suggestion is helpful, but unnecessarily discrete. A metaphor for what? In this reading, Kundry's "wound" could be her passionate sexual

---

[136] http://www.monsalvat.no/trans0.htm.

desire for Parsifal. Or it could stand—along the lines we have outlined—more explicitly for the vagina, a metaphor by no means unique to Wagner.

Parsifal offers "the sinner" redemption. Kundry replies that her redemption would lie in making love to him. "Love and redemption will be your reward[137] if you show me the way to Amfortas," Parsifal answers.

But Kundry, "breaking out in rage," tells him he will never find the way to that "luster after shame, whom I ridiculed—laughed at—laughed at! Ha ha!, he was wounded with his own spear!"[138] Kundry's malicious laughter here echoes her laughter at the suffering Christ ages and ages ago.

In *Mein Leben,* Wagner reccalls his childhood fantasy of assuming the place of the crucified Christ on the Cross. "The boy, who only a few years before had gazed in agonizing desire at the altarpiece of the Kreuzkirche, and in ecstatic fervor had wished himself in the place of the Redeemer on the Cross, had already so far lost his reverence for the priest to whom he went for lessons preparatory to Confirmation, that he was not loath to join in ridicule of him, and even, in league with his comrades, ate up a portion of the offering intended for [the priest] in goodies."[139] This

---

137 "lohnen" ("reward," or "repay") is the word in the text printed in *Gesammelte Schriften und Dichtungen von Richard Wagner*, (Leipzig, 1871).

138 "den Unsel'gen, Schmachlüsternen, den ich verlachte—lachte—lachte! Haha! Ihn traf ja der eig'ne Speer!"

139 My trans. "Der Knabe, der noch vor wenigen Jahren mit schmerzlicher Sehnsucht nach dem Altarblatte der Kreuzkirche geblickt, und in extatischer Begeisterung sich an die Stelle des Erlösers am Kreuze gewünscht, hatte die Hochachtung vor dem Geistlichen, zu welchem er in die der Confirmations vorangehenden Vorbereitungsstunden ging,

memory casts an autobiographical shadow across the figure of Kundry. As Kundry had laughed at the suffering Christ, Wagner joined in mockery of his priest. Wagner identified with Kundry as he did with the Flying Dutchman and the figure of the Wandering Jew. The wound Kundry here derides was inflicted, she tells Parsifal, by the same person whose curse lends her her own powers, and she will summon up the identical punishment against him should he show compassion to "the sinner," Amfortas.

But her mood turns suddenly pleading again. "Compassion! Compassion for me! Be mine for just one hour! Just one hour yours—and you shall be led on the way!"

Kundry attempts to embrace him, but Parsifal "pushes her forcefully from him." "Go, unfortunate woman!"

Resigned, finally, to the futility of her suit, Kundry calls upon Klingsor and his enthralled knights to bar Parsifal's way. She promises darkly that, "should you flee from here, and find all the paths in the world, the [one] path you seek you will not find, for ways and byways that lead away from me, I curse them for you: wander! wander!"[140] And she commits Parsifal to Klingsor's evil power. Klingsor appears on the ramparts of the castle, and hurls the holy spear at Parsifal, the fool. Miraculously, the spear stops short in mid-

---

bereits so sehr verloren, dass er zu seiner Verspottung nicht ungern sich gesellte, und sogar einen Theil des für ihn bestimmten Beichtgeldes in Uebereinstimmung mit einer hierzu verbundenen Genossenschaft vernaschte." *Mein Leben*, (München, 1911), p. 29.

[140] "Irre! Irre!" The German verb "irren" means not only to wander, roam, or stray, but also to be in error, to be wrong, morally and intellectually.

flight, hovering over Parsifal's head, a sudden stay that mirrors the hero's timely retreat from Kundry's fateful kiss. He seizes the spear "with his hand," holding it aloft. Then waving the spear in the sign of the Cross, he causes the castle to collapse and sink "as though in an earthquake." The magic flower garden withers to a barren desert.

Hastening off, Parsifal turns briefly to address his curious parting words to Kundry, "You know where you can find me again!" Or, as printed in the *Gesammelte Schriften und Dichtungen,* "You know where—only—you will see me again!"[141]

[141] "Du weißt wo einzig du mich wiedersieh'st!" an interesting word-play on the colloquial German farewell, "auf Wiedersehen."

IV: Holy Spear and Grail

Act III brings us back both to the pastoral "domain of the Grail,"[142] and later to the temple where the revelation rite will take place, as in Act I. The structure of *Parsifal* might be said to be more architectural than that of *The Ring*, for example, which, though it ends where it began in the Rhine, to be sure, nonetheless is driven narratively forward towards its cataclysmic conclusion. *Parsifal*, by contrast, resembles a triptych more than a saga, with Act II its central panel, and Acts I and III its side-panels. Accordingly, there is less forward narrative thrust towards a dramatic conclusion. In fact, *Parsifal*'s shattering climax occurs rather at its mid-point, in Act II than at its end, so that the work's structure invites simultaneous contemplation of the whole. "Time becomes space," in the words of Gurnemanz; the story unfolds of necessity in the temporal dimension, but at so measured a pace that once returned to the landscape of Monsalvat in Act III, we feel almost as though we have never left. This architectural symmetry is underscored by Wagner's stage directions. In Act I, he has specified: "Gradually . . . the stage transforms itself from left to right." For the transformation sequence of Act III from floral

---

142 "Im Gebiete des Grals"

meadow to Temple of the Grail he directs: "The setting transforms itself very gradually as in the first act, only from right to left,"[143] as though we stood viewing the two facing wings of an altarpiece.

The prelude to Act III reflects this mirror-image symmetry musically. We do not begin in the tranquil mood as of the Good Friday music later in the Act, but with melancholy and even anxious variations of themes—leitmotifs, if you will—to which we have earlier been introduced. Even the Dresden Amen, which in its native form constitutes so definitive a concluding cadence appears here midway through the prelude twice, in pointedly unresolved form. It occurs once more similarly unresolved as though to herald Kundry's inarticulate scream in response to Gurnemanz's restoring her to waking life. "As she finally opens her eyes, she lets out a scream."[144] The anxious tenor of the Act III Prelude stands in striking contrast to the ethereal calm pervading the Prelude to Act I, pronounced even in sections in the minor mode, and prevailing until the extended tremolo in the violins towards the conclusion hints vaguely at forthcoming tensions and conflict. Thus, the Prelude to Act III reflects the turmoil of the preceding, adjacent Act II, and only later are we returned symmetrically to the transcendent mood with which *Parsifal* began.

The setting of Act III is at the edge of the forest in the

---

143 "Die Gegend verwandelt sich sehr allmählich, ähnlicherweise wie im ersten Aufzuge, nur von rechts nach links." The stage directions to Act I read: "Allmählich . . . verwandelt sich die Bühne, von links nach rechts hin . . ."

144 "Als sie die Augen endlich öffnet, stößt sie einen Schrei aus."

domain of the Grail; a flowery meadow stretches towards the background. This tranquil flowery meadow (though parallel) presents a graphic counter to Klingsor's insidious flowers in Act II. Parsifal himself notes this parallelism when he exclaims, "How beautiful the meadow seems to me today! Indeed, I did encounter wondrous flowers that, craving,[145] entwined me up to my head; but never did I see such mild and tender grasses, blossoms, and flowers, nor did they all smell so childlike sweet, nor so charmingly speak intimately to me." How different from those carnal flowers he "saw wither, who once laughed for me: do they long today for redemption?" The licentious laughter of Klingsor's flowers is contrasted with the chaste laughter of those he now beholds, and it is Kundry's tears of remorse that effect this magic: "Your tears, too, turned into the dew of grace: You wept!—look! the meadow is laughing."[146] Parsifal kisses Kundry "gently on the forehead," to the sound of bells in the distance. This kiss is not only the obverse of Kundry's fateful kiss in Act II, it is also an enactment of the ritual "kiss of peace" of the Christian churches, in German, "der heilige Kuß."

This flowery meadow represents a counterpoise to Klingsor's garden. Gurnemanz tells Parsifal, "Sir! That is . . . Good Friday magic."[147] Categorically opposite Klingsor's sorcery, this is the redemptive miracle of compassion.

---

145 "süchtig"

146 "Auch deine Träne ward zum Segenstaue: du weinest!—sieh! es lacht die Aue."

147 "Karfreitagszauber"

New in this setting, we note, is the holy spring ("Quell"), [148] of which we shall have more to say shortly. If Klingsor's magic garden is infused with the feminine symbolism of the "garden enclosed" of the *Song of Solomon*, this flowing spring is similarly charged. As Derrick Everett observes in his marginal commentary, "Stage designers should note that a spring and a stream are important elements of this scene, in which water plays a symbolic role. A jug of holy water is a poor substitute."[149]

The day, then, is Good Friday, anniversary of the crucifixion of The Redeemer (never explicitly named Christ in *Parsifal*). Gurnemanz appears from his hermit's hut as a visibly aged man, indicative of how many years Parsifal has been on his arduous quest. Had Wagner chosen to give us a saga in the manner of Wolfram von Eschenbach and the other Grail romances of the Middle Ages, he would have had to present a rambling sequence of Parsifal's adventures along the route of his quest. In a May 30, 1859 letter to Mathilde Wesendonck, Wagner had actually disparaged Wolfram's vapid stringing together of such knightly exploits. Instead, in *Parsifal*, these adventures are referenced only obliquely and in the vaguest of generalities.

"I came along a path of error and suffering,"[150] Parsifal tells Gurnemanz. Lest it be desecrated, he dared not fight his battles with the holy spear he was bearing back to the Grail

---

[148] This masculine form is a poetic (and archaic) variant of the more usual feminine "Quelle."

[149] Everett, *op. cit.*

[150] "Der Irrnis und der Leiden Pfade kam ich." "Irrnis" denotes both wandering and error, both directional, moral, and intellectual, and thus cannot be easily rendered in English translation. Cf. footnote 140, p. 67.

Knighthood, and this protective deference cost him "wounds from every weapon." To Gurnemanz's question whom he sought, Parsifal indicates (without naming him) Amfortas, to bring him healing. "But oh! a wild curse drove me about in trackless wandering, never to find the way of healing: countless troubles, battles, and disputes forced me off the path, though I thought I knew it."[151] In this nutshell, Parsifal sums up his arduous, years-long journey whose object was the return of the holy spear to the Knights of Montsalvat. Little more is said of the plethora of adventures that conventionally form the narrative substance of the medieval Grail romances.

The act has begun with Kundry's inarticulate moan, the first human sound we hear following the prelude. Gurnemanz discovers her lying in a thicket of thorns. In an echo of the "death-sleep" in which Klingsor had kept her as sex slave, he cries, "Awake! Awake to spring! Cold and stiff! This time I truly thought she was dead . . . You mad woman! Have you no word for me? Is this the thanks for my once more having waked you out of the death-sleep?" The word is "Todesschlafe." It is repeated several lines later when Gurnemanz attributes his ability to wake her from the "death-sleep" ("Todesschlafe") to the grace immanent in the day, Good Friday, and it is the same word Klingsor has used at the beginning of Act II to describe the coma-like state in which he warehouses Kundry, from which he awakens her when he requires her dubious services. Its use here in Act III

[151] "Doch—ach! -den Weg des Heiles nie zu finden, in pfadlosen Irren trieb ein wilder Fluch mich umher: zahlose Nöte, Kämpfe, und Streite zwangen mich ab vom Pfade, wähnt' ich ihn recht schon erkannt."

might not suggest the theme of necrophilia were it not for its echo of that more obviously freighted usage in Act II. If that theme is thus adumbrated here, it testifies to the fact that throughout *Parsifal,* the purportedly spiritual dimension is deeply informed throughout by the corporeal, and by instinctual drives that, though repressed from consciousness, nonetheless manifest themselves symbolically—or in clinical terms, in "symptom formation."

Kundry's first, hoarse, articulate words are "Service . . . service!,"[152] and are surely in allusion to the words of Jesus in the *Gospel of Mark,* ". . . whoever would be first must be servant of all. For even the Son of Man did not come to be served, but to serve, and to give his life as a ransom for many."[153] The theme of service is continued when Kundry washes Parsifal's feet—an echo of Jesus's washing his disciples' feet at the Last Supper.

> But before the Passover, as Jesus knew that his time had come, that he was to go out of this world to the Father: as he had loved his own, who were in the world, he loved them to the end.
> And at the supper, when the devil had already inspired Judas, the son of Simon Iscariot, to betray him,

---

152 "Dienen . . . Dienen!"

153 *Mark* 10: 44-5, ". . . welcher will groß werden unter euch, der soll euer Diener sein; und welcher unter euch will der Vornehmste werden, der soll aller Knecht sein. Denn auch des Menschen Sohn ist nicht gekommen, daß er sich dienen lasse, sondern daß er diene und gebe sein Leben zur Bezahlung für viele."

and Jesus knew that the Father had put all things into his hands, and that he had come from God and was going to God:
he stood up from the supper, took off his clothes, and wrapped a cloth around his waist.
After that, he poured water into a basin and began to wash his disciples' feet, drying them with the cloth that was wrapped around him.
He came then to Simon Peter, and he spoke to him, "Lord, are you going to wash my feet?"
Jesus answered and said to him: "You do not know now what I am doing; but later you will understand."
Then Peter spoke to him: "Never shall you wash my feet." Jesus answered him: "Unless I wash you, you have no part with me." . . .
When now he had washed their feet, he put on his clothes and sat down again and spoke to them once more: "Do you understand what I have done for you?"
"You call me 'Teacher' and 'Lord,' and speak rightly in this, for I am that truly.
Now that I, your Lord and Teacher, have washed your feet, you also should wash one another's feet.
I have set you an example that you should do as I have done for you.
Verily, verily I say to you, the servant is not greater than his master, nor is the apostle greater than the one who sent him."[154]

---

[154] *John* 13: 1-16, my trans. of the Lutheran text.

Similarly, Kundry anoints Parsifal's feet with the precious contents of a small golden bottle, echoing the consecrating act of the woman in Bethany (*Matthew* 26: 6-13) who anoints the head of Jesus with "precious liquid" from a "glass" (in Luther's translation). The apostles are indignant over what they see as a senseless waste. Jesus chides them, saying, "This woman . . . has done me a good work. The poor you have with you always; me, though, you do not have always . . . Verily I say unto you: wherever this gospel is preached throughout the entire world, it will also be told in her memory what she has done." Luther's words were of course memorably set in Bach's *St. Matthew Passion.* Whether Bach's music was in the back of Wagner's mind at this point in his own composition we cannot know. The consecration is completed by Gurnemanz who anoints Parsifal's head with the remainder of the precious water.

Consistent with the architectural symmetry of *Parsifal,* in which Act III mirrors Act I, Gurnemanz has posed questions Parsifal cannot answer. "Do you not know, then, how holy a day today is?" Parsifal mutely shakes his head. "Where, then, do you come from? With what heathens have you abided that you do not know today is the most holy Good Friday?"

By way of remorseful response, Parsifal mutely bows his head further. "Do not give affront to the Lord, who today, lacking all weapons, gave his holy blood to the sinful world for its atonement," says Gurnemanz, instructing him to quickly put aside his weapons. Parsifal sticks the spear into the ground, lays sword and shield beside it, and removes his helmet.

In pouring the remaining "precious water" on Parsifal's head, Gurnemanz anoints him the new Grail King, who will replace Amfortas in his office of revealing the Grail. Parsifal's first act as Grail King, in turn, is to take water from the holy spring and sprinkle it on Kundry's head, baptizing her. This mutual anointing serves the ever more apparent identity of Parsifal and Kundry: from this point to the end of the act, they represent an increasingly single androgynous entity, foreshadowed in Act I by the image of the male and female swan couple circling and blessing the holy lake of the Grail, which Gurnemanz had evoked in his reproach of Parsifal's senseless act with his bow and arrow. This is an identity more total even than marriage, and it is symbolized in the imminent reuniting of phallic spear and vaginal Grail.

We note in passing a parallel to *Das Rheingold* here. The Grail actually feeds the Knights of Montsalvat; they depend on the ritual of uncovering and revealing the Grail for their sustenance. Because Amfortas—to spare himself the further pain of witnessing the Grail—has selfishly refused to continue enacting the rite, the Knights languish, and are compelled to forage for herbs and roots to maintain a bare subsistence. "The holy nourishment [of Eucharist] is now denied us," Gurnemanz tells Parsifal, who has remarked that everything in the Grail's domain seems somehow changed. "Common fodder must sustain us; whereby our heroes' vitality has dried up[155] . . . pale and wretched, the dispirited and leaderless Knighthood staggers about." This picture of a Knighthood sapped of vitality parallels the

---

155 The "drying up" ("Versiegung") of the heroes' vitality is consistent with the wide range of fluid imagery of *Parsifal.*

pathetic state of the gods of *Das Rheingold* when—Freya held captive by the giants—they are denied the rejuvenating nourishment of her divine apples.

The malaise that has spread over the realm of the Grail, tied to the physical incapacity and sexual impotence of the Grail King, is a feature common to *Parsifal*'s medieval sources, in which typically not just the King's retinue but the land itself is laid barren, fruitless—a wasteland.[156] Now, however, even before the renewed observance of the Grail rite brings redemption to the Grail realm, the flowery meadow of Act III manifests a sign, an emblem of rebirth and fertility: "field and meadow" are watered with the life-giving tears of the remorse of sinners. "Now, every creature is glad for this sweet sign of the Redeemer." For this day, no human foot will tread the grasses and flowers on the meadow; in imitation of God's compassion, "this day, man will walk with pious grace, protecting them with gentle tread."[157]

Parenthetically, we should observe that in rather short order, from knight errant adrift down myriad false paths, Parsifal has been elevated to Grail King and high priest of Montsalvat. Most of the narrative steps that would ordinarily be required to make so extraordinary a transition credible are blithely glossed over here in Act III of *Parsifal*. Swept along on the flood of Wagner's ethereal score, though, the audience will not even miss this narrative connective tissue, or find the transition illogical. This is because we are in the realm of allegory, where we do not necessarily look

---

156 T .S. Eliot based his poem on this imagery.

157 "der Mensch auch heut' in frommer Huld sie schont mit sanftem Schritt."

for meaning, or logical continuity, or even coherence in surface narrative. Nor is there any point in analyzing character, behavior, or feelings psychologically. As human figures, the *dramatis personae* of *Parsifal* have no psychological reality. This is not Shakespeare. On the apparent level, these figures are paste-board. Whatever meanings are to be found in the work lie on altogether different (not necessarily higher) planes.

To hallow Titurel's funeral, Amfortas, in expiation of his father's death, has agreed to administer the Grail rite one last time. Parsifal's appearance in the domain of the Grail bearing the holy spear has been fortuitous, then. Gurnemanz perceives that "yet today" he will perform "a high work[158] . . . in celebrating a holy office." For this duty, he must be "immaculate,"[159] and the dust of his long journey[160] must be washed from him. "The holy spring itself [shall be] our pilgrim's reinvigorating bath." Parsifal is led by both Gurnemanz and Kundry to the spring, where they remove his armor and bathe him: in essence, as we have seen, a baptism, which serves simultaneously as the anointing of Parsifal as Grail King.

Gurnemanz announces: "Midday. The hour is here." And now the relation between mentor and acolyte has been entirely reversed, echoing the words of Jesus cited above, as

---

[158] "ein hohes Werk"

[159] "fleckenrein"

[160] Wagner's word is "Irrfahrt," whose connotations, as we have seen, are untranslatable because of the word's multivalence. The constituent verb, "irren," suggests not only the meaning "wandering, or odyssey," but also "gone astray," with its relevant moral implications. See footnote 140, p. 67.

well as his words from *Matthew* 19:30 and 20: 16 that the first shall be last, and the last, first.[161] "Permit, Lord, that your servant escort you!" The stage transforms from forest edge and flowery mead to Temple of the Grail. The rite to be celebrated is a dual one: funeral and sacrament.

One group of knights carries the grail in its shrine; another group bears in the coffin holding the body of the father of Amfortas, Titurel. Amfortas apostrophizes his father's body, begging him to intercede on his behalf with "the Redeemer" to grant him the death he longs for, and with it, an end to his suffering from "the horrible wound, the poison that eats at his heart."

The knights press him: "Uncover the Grail! Perform the office! Your father admonishes you: you must! You must!" But Amfortas, reneging on his pledge is adamant.

"No! No more! Ha! Already I feel death's night descend, and you wish me once more to return to life? [You are] mad! Who wants to force me to live? If only you could give me death!" He tears open his gown. "Here I am—the open wound, here! Here flows my blood which poisons me. Take out your weapons! Plunge your swords, deep—deep, to the hilt! Up! You heroes! Kill the sinner and his torment; perhaps then on its own the Grail will glow for you!"

In the matrix of corporeal symbolism we have established in this work, Amfortas presents an emblematic fantasy of violent sexual congress: the bleeding vaginal "wound" penetrated by the phallic swords of the knights, a fantasy

---

161 "Also werden die Letzten die Ersten und die Ersten die Letzten sein."

consistent with the work's pervasive theme identified at the outset: sex as perilous, a residue of the primal scene, in which parental sex is perceived by the child as doing injury to one or both participants. The fantasy suggests further that the profusely bleeding vaginal wound represents menstruation, an association reinforced by the ensuing vision of Parsifal, who steps in to perform his redemptive healing act.

"Only one weapon serves: the wound can be closed only by the spear that struck it,"[162] he cries. Though on examination, the logic of this assertion is obscure, even dubious, we accept it in the climactic rush of this final scene. Its actual logic lies not on the narrative level, but on the symbolic level, whether this be understood spiritually or sexually. He touches the wound with the tip of the spear, and the wound is miraculously healed. In one of the work's most stirring passages—musically, dramatically, and poetically—Parsifal proclaims, "The holy spear, I bring it back to you!"[163] Holding the spear aloft, he looks up at its tip, rhapsodizing, "From it I see holy blood flowing in desire for its sibling fountain, flowing there in the surge of the Grail."[164]

The "sibling fountain" in Parsifal's vision here connects the flow of blood from the tip of the spear to the baptismal liquid flowing from the holy spring so prominent in the earlier action of Act III. The word for both is "Quelle,"

---

162 "Nur eine Waffe taugt: die Wunde schließt der Speer nur, der sie schlug."

163 "Den heil'gen Speer—ich bring' ihn euch zurück!"

164 "ihm seh' ich heil'ges Blut entfließen in Sehnsucht nach dem verwandten Quelle, der dort fließt in des Grales Welle."

which denotes both spring and fountain. Though the sacramental water flowing from the holy spring is a clear liquid, it comes now to partake of all the symbolic resonance of the blood so pervading *Parsifal.*

We have noted the broad critical agreement that the imagery of spear and Grail is distinctly gendered. This fantasy of the phallic spear bleeding from its tip suggests first of all a genital wound, in keeping with the ideation of the primal scene. Second, genital bleeding is itself suggestive of menstruation. If the phallic spear is gendered—as it obviously is—the image might hint at the fantasy of male menstruation.[165] More important, though, the confusion of blood and semen inherent in the image of the spear bleeding from its tip mirrors the union of spear and Grail, which in turn symbolizes the merger of identities of Parsifal and Kundry. The dramatic tension of the entire work, that is, the quest for redemption, is resolved in this androgynous union.

In this context, we might cite Paul to the *Galatians* (3: 28): "There is neither Jew nor Greek, there is neither bond nor free, there is neither male nor female: for ye are all one in Christ Jesus."[166] Wagner admired the Pauline Epistles, regarded Paul as "the first Christian,"[167] and was impressed by the profound influence of Paul on Luther.[168] More

---

165 Poul M. Faergeman, "Fantasies of Menstruation in Men," *Psychoanalytic Quarterly* 24 (1955), pp. 1-19. Such a fantasy is equally evident in the image (above) of Amfortas's profusely bleeding lateral wound.

166 "Hier ist kein Jude noch Grieche, hier ist kein Knecht noch Freier, hier ist kein Mann noch Weib; denn ihr seid allzumal einer in Christo Jesu."

167 Cosima Wagner, *Diaries*, May 3, 1882.

168 *Ibid.*, Nov. 8. 1878.

directly, in an entry of 1880, Cosima records that Wagner ". . . plays the first theme of *Parsifal* to himself and, returning, explains how he gave the words to a chorus so the effect would be neither feminine nor masculine, Christ should be quite genderless, neither woman nor man; thus Leonardo, too, in the Last Supper, tried to present an almost feminine face with a beard."[169]

On a deeper psychological level, we see at work here Wagner's own well-known and documented proclivity towards assuming female identity: his penchant for dressing in women's clothes, his requirements for silk undergarments (purportedly to accommodate the sensitivity of his skin brought on by life-long erysipelas), his love of perfumed baths and florid, flamboyant décor. ". . . This high-minded composer of monumental music dramas was also a sybarite on a grand scale, with a particular penchant for silks and satins. From his violet velvet drapes to his pink silk underwear, his tastes became the stuff of the gossip sheets and satirical cartoons," writes Barry Millington.[170]

Joachim Köhler paints a similar picture: ". . . He wore tailor-made silk underwear and elegant indoor clothing decorated with all manner of ruches, tassels and rosettes that seem more in keeping with a woman's wardrobe than a man's. He also had negligees made to his own designs, dressing gowns of a kind that Madame de Pompadour might well have worn, and even in Bayreuth he read Paris fashion

---

[169] *Ibid.*, June 27, 1880.

[170] Barry Millington, *The Sorcerer of Bayreuth: Richard Wagner, his Work and his World*, (Oxford, 2012), ; 149. See Millington, *op. cit.*, pp. 151-158 for the extensive profile of this aspect of Wagner's character.

magazines in order to keep abreast of the latest trends. The ladies' drawers, undershirts and colourful Russia leather bootees may have recalled his childhood with sisters whose 'more delicate wardrobe items,' as he confessed in his autobiography, cast a 'subtly exciting spell' on his imagination from a very early age. In order to be really 'happy,' all he then needed was maternal affection . . . Needless to say, Wagner wore women's clothing only when he was alone, and whenever he was caught *in flagrante* by his wives, he always had an excuse."[171]

Although at this remove much about Wagner's conscious and unconscious gender ambivalence is unknowable, it is safe to say that the cross-gender behavior and ideation sketched out by Millington and Köhler reveal a psychic struggle that surely occasioned significant anxiety: to borrow Charles Brenner's trenchant title, we see a "mind in conflict."[172] The exact mechanics of how Wagner's gender ambivalence meshed with Oedipal conflict is certainly beyond the scope of this study, and perhaps beyond the competence of even a trained psychoanalyst. It is safe to say, though, that these two streams of conflict must have been intertwined.

The relationship between Parsifal and Kundry is, then, a projection of such conflict, and the androgynous synthesis of their relationship in *Parsifal*'s denouement constitutes a

---

171 Joachim Köhler, *Richard Wagner: The Last of the Titans*, (Yale, 2004), pp. 454-5. For the extensive profile of this aspect of Wagner's character, see Köhler, *op. cit.*, pp. 453-6.

172 Charles Brenner, M.D., *The Mind in Conflict*, (International Universities Press, 1982).

resolution in fantasy whose aim is the allaying of anxiety.[173] Gazing rapturously up at Parsifal, Kundry sinks expiring[174] to the ground, her being essentially dissolving into his, recapitulating Herzeleide's death Kundry had announced in Act I, and conforming to Freud's "Ur-motif" of the mother who sacrifices herself in initiating the son to sexual intercourse. Kundry has effected this initiation quite literally. Although Parsifal retreated from the brink of penetration, we can legitimately consider this congress an instance of *coitus interruptus,* and Parsifal has come away from it miraculously enlightened. At bottom, the fantasy is resolution of both gender ambivalence and the Oedipus Complex—miraculously achieving union (or reunion) with the mother while artfully dodging the punishment of castration. We might dub it *coitus immaculatus*.

"Highest wonder of salvation!" intones the choir of boys, squires, and knights. "Redemption to the Redeemer." Though this formula, "Erlösung dem Erlöser!" is thought enigmatic, we see now that it is really quite transparent. It cannot refer to Christ, who requires no redemption, but refers unambiguously to Parsifal, whose quest throughout has been for the redemption now achieved, essentially in androgynous union with Kundry. "Durch Mitleid,

---

173 Otto Rank, *op.cit.*, pp. 104-5, writes, ". . . The myths of world-creation and of 'world-parents,' [have], in the process of cosmic assimilation, . . . preserved for us the most sublime attempts to 'undo' the birth trauma, to deny the separation from the mother." This is of course distinct from (though related to, and certainly not mutually exclusive with) the castration anxiety attendant on witnessing the primal scene.

174 Wagner's word in the stage directions is "entseelt," a poetic euphemism for "dying" whose literal meaning is "soul-extracted."

wissend,"[175] by experiencing the wound of Amfortas in Kundry's kiss, he has transcended his native "foolishness," gained knowledge without quite lapsing into sin, become the Redeemer, and fulfilled the prophecy of his coming foretold to Titurel. The Grail glows at its brightest intensity of sanguine red as a dove descends and hovers over the site of the ritual. The dove is no doubt derived from that avatar of the Holy Spirit at the baptism of Jesus: ". . . and behold, the heavens opened above him. And he saw the Spirit of God like a dove descend and come above him. And behold, a voice from heaven that spoke: This is my beloved son, in whom I delight."[176] Whether we should additionally read some underlying "Freudian" signification into the symbol of the dove[177] is of no great consequence since the psychoanalytic arc of *Parsifal* is clear by now regardless of this final detail.

---

[175] "Through compassion, knowing."

[176] ". . . und siehe, da tat sich der Himmel auf über ihm. Und er sah den Geist Gottes gleich als eine Taube herabfahren und über ihn kommen. Und siehe, eine Stimme vom Himmel herab sprach: Dies ist mein Sohn, an welchem ich Wohlgefallen habe." *Matthew* 3: 16, 17. Virtually the same narrative appears in *Luke* 3: 22.

[177] Freud interpreted birds in dreams generally as phallic, and their flight as sexual intercourse..

V: Inside Out

If the Parsifal/Kundry pair is emblematic of inner conflict and its resolution in fantasy, we can go a step further, I think, and see the entire *dramatis personae* of *Parsifal* as a projection of Wagner's collective inner life—not, as I have said, in any sense leading to a definitive psychoanalysis of the artist, but as a psychic snapshot in time. I argue similarly in *The Wagner Complex* that the world of *The Ring* can be seen as a dynamic tableau of the Wagnerian psyche, comprising its introjected agencies, or "objects." Most important, we should always bear in mind that our interest and our focus is on *Parsifal,* the work, not on Wagner the man and artist. The present study remains literary/critical, not psycho-biographical. To the extent we have recourse to and interpret biographical data, it is to elucidate the work. Whether and how, viewed in the present psychoanalytic light, the work in turn sheds light on the biography is matter for quite another study.

It cannot be stressed too strongly that adopting such a psychoanalytic view of the work, is by no means to suggest displacing other more straight-forward analyses of the *Parsifal* narrative, in the manner of some medieval writers who, comparing allegory to a nut, exhorted their readers to discard the shell of the nut once the true, spiritual kernel of meaning had been revealed. On the contrary, understanding the unconscious streams of meaning pervading a work simply allows for a richer experience of its surface narrative. As we have noted, in any complex work of art, meanings are vertically layered. Aesthetic experience is richest when these layers can be apprehended simultaneously—the whole nut, so to speak.

By the same token, I would never urge that stage productions of *Parsifal* be based on such psychoanalytic levels of interpretation. Quite to the contrary. *Those unconscious meanings either inhere in the work, or they do not.* Let the work speak for itself. That is precisely why the present study has proceeded methodically through the literary text, exploring the resonances of Wagner's actual words. A stage production should hew to Wagner's intentions, spelled out in his explicit stage directions. To take one specific example, although as we have seen, unconscious imagery of menstruation informs the blood motif throughout *Parsifal,* it would be a mistake to manifest this fantasy in any literal sense in staging the work—by suffusing the stage with obviously menstrual blood for example. I am personally conservative in the matter of staging Wagner's works. Wagner knew what he wanted, and spelled it out clearly.

We earlier chose to eschew the thickets of object relations theory in favor of exegetical clarity in the present study, and once again we'll adopt a more informal and intuitive approach to the idea that the *dramatis personae* of *Parsifal* may be viewed as comprising the myriad figures populating its author's inner life. All the emotionally significant people in his early life—in psychoanalytic terms, "objects," that is, objects of the drives—exist not only in the "real" world externally, but also as introjected figures—often split into multiple and conflicting aspects—in his inner mental world. That inner world, peopled by all these cathected figures, is characterized by fluidity and ambivalence. Thus, these introjected figures easily transmogrify and are invested with seemingly contradictory valences, like figures in a dream. It is best not to be rigidly doctrinaire in their interpretation.

So we see two mother figures, Herzeleide and Kundry, quite distinct one from the other, but representing different aspects of the maternal principle, and representing, more specifically, the subject's (our fictional Wagner's[178]) ambivalent relation to the maternal. Likewise, more than one figure plays the role of the father: Gurnemanz, Titurel, Amfortas, and Klingsor. Each represents a different aspect of the paternal image; taken as a group, they embody profound ambivalence towards the father. In fact the figure of Amfortas embodies the subject himself every bit as much as the subject's introjected father; similarly, in androgynous union with Parsifal, Kundry comes to embody the subject himself no less than his mother.

---

[178] When we speak of "Wagner" in the present context, we mean the authorial consciousness projected in the work. Though this "character" is obviously derived from the historical Richard Wagner, he must be regarded as essentially as fictional an entity as *Parsifal* itself, if for no other reason than that as a projected representation of its author, *Parsifal* is so in the nature of a snapshot in time, whereas an actual, analyzable personality has a history.

Though this reading may lay itself open to the critique that in psychoanalytic exegesis nothing can have real meaning because anything can be seen to mean anything,[179] the arbitrariness and confusion of the inner symbolic fluidity we have sketched out is really only apparent. The confusion is resolved the moment we recognize that all the figures of the *dramatis personae* collectively *are* this fictional Wagner, fixed in a moment of time. We might dispute the attribution of particular traits to one character or another, but such differences assume lesser significance if collectively all the traits refer to a single personality.

That the Wagnerian psyche was complex, chock full of ambivalence and contradiction is hardly in dispute. If we picture this psyche as a balloon, filled with such a plethora of figures ("objects," if you will) making up Wagner's interior world, and then imagine this balloon turned inside out so that suddenly these introjected figures act out their roles in a simulacrum of the external world, we have an idea of *Parsifal* as the projected representation of its author's inner self.

In summary, then, to Parsifal, Gurnemanz has posed the primal question: *Weißt du was du sahst*? Do you know what you saw? This question is an enigma whose solution becomes the goal of the "pure fool's" arduous quest. The answer—the primal scene—is experienced by our hero in the flesh viscerally and shatteringly in Kundry's passionate embrace. The emotional sequelae following upon that erotic enlightenment—guilt, remorse, compassion, and finally

---

179 See footnote 124, p. 58.

absolution—constitute the measured denouement of *Parsifal,* which culminates in a fantasy of redemption and resolution of primal anxiety.

Wagner's initial sense of Wolfram's *Parzival* material had been dark indeed. As he wrote Mathilde Wesendonck on May 30, 1859, (at that stage) he regarded Amfortas as the principal figure of the drama—the unending agony of his lateral wound as an almost unbearable heightening of the tragic Act III of *Tristan und Isolde.* With the gradual evolution of Parsifal's enlightenment and redemption as the central focus of the work, however, and the role of Amfortas relegated from a principal to a supporting one, the whole tenor of the work was radically, diametrically transformed. Whereas *The Ring* concludes in bleak Schopenhauerian pessimism, *Parsifal,* Wagner's sublime farewell to the stage and the world, ascends to its hopeful—albeit wishful—resolution on the wings of that dove hovering over the Temple of the Grail.

ABOUT THE AUTHOR

Tom Artin was educated at Princeton University, from which he holds a B.A. in English Literature, and a Ph. D. in Comparative Medieval Literature. Previous books are *The Allegory of Adventure,* a study of Arthurian Romances by Chrétien de Troyes; *Earth Talk: Independent Voices on the Environment*; and *The Wagner Complex: Genesis and Meaning of The Ring*. He is the translator of numerous books, primarily from German, most recently *The Laughing Wagner*. Tom lives with his wife, Cynthia, in the village of Sparkill, in New York's Hudson Valley.

Made in the USA
Charleston, SC
13 June 2016